☆

*A*merica, September 11th
The **Courage** *to* **Give**

☆

$\mathcal{A}$merica, September 11th
The Courage to Give

The Triumph of the Human Spirit

Edited by Jackie Waldman
with Brenda Welchlin
and Karen Frost

Remember our Carage to Give

— Karen Frost

CONARI PRESS
Berkeley, California

Conari Press books are distributed by Publishers Group West.

Cover Photography: AP/Wide World Photos
Cover and Book Design: Suzanne Albertson

Library of Congress Cataloging-in-Publication Data

America September 11 : the courage to give / edited by Jackie Waldman
with Brenda Welchlin and Karen Frost.
p.   cm.
ISBN 1-57324-816-9
1. September 11 Terrorist Attacks, 2001.
2. Victims of terrorism—Services for—United States.
3. Voluntarism—United States.
4. Helping behavior—United States. 5. Generosity. 6. Courage.
I. Waldman, Jackie. II. Welchlin, Brenda. III. Frost, Karen.

HV6432 .A5 2001
362.88—dc21   2001006189

ISBN: 1-57324-816-9

Printed in the United States of America on recycled paper.

01 02 03   10 9 8 7 6 5 4 3 2 1

*T*o the lives lost, the victims' loved ones,
the invincible spirit of mankind,
and an inexhaustible capacity to give

America, September 11th

*T*his book is arriving at bookstores shortly after the events it describes. The usual reason for what passes as haste in book publishing is to "strike while the market is hot." That is decidedly not our purpose here. Not a single business or individual, from the author and agent to the publisher, printer, and distributor is making a single penny from this book. All involved have agreed to forgo any profit and turn all net proceeds over to the American Red Cross and the New York Firefighters 9-11 Disaster Relief Fund.

We did, however, feel that the extraordinary outpouring of strength, courage, compassion, and generosity that has emerged from this tragedy has forged a powerful sense of community and connection that cries out for documentation. We believe that these stories and the thousands of others that they represent are a clear and unmistakable announcement of a deep and significant new chapter in our history.

We believe that when people look back on these events later, the greatest impact will come not from the war on terrorism itself, but from the considerably more subtle and powerful changes to the human heart that are sweeping across the globe. When trying to capture in words the power of that change, participants have routinely referred to an extraordinary "coming together." It is, in a very real sense, the beginning of a true coming together, an awareness struck deep in the heart, that all of us, from every land, every race, and every religion, are truly in this together.

Stephanie Kriner

THE SPIRIT OF AMERICA
Courage and Faith

*T*his terrible tragedy has touched all of us in a permanent way. America's spirit, our liberty, and our national security have been attacked. Unfair and inexplicable, the events have created an extraordinary imprint on the mind, the body, and the spirit of a family, a community, and a nation.

America has been changed forever, but our sturdy foundations are unchanged. In the midst of the overpowering grief that envelops us all, the sadness, the loss we feel, there is strength, and there is unity. After all, America is built on an idea—of freedom and community spirit.

The resilience and dignity of Americans is renowned. In the midst of so much grief, America has pulled together. The American Red Cross is privileged to serve the American people at this time of great human need—and provide a concrete way for people to help themselves and help each other.

Everyone is asking, "What can I do?" There is much to do in the weeks and months ahead. Reach out to your neighbor, console a grieving friend, give blood, volunteer in your community, or make a donation to your charity of choice. Most of all—sustain this spirit of America at its best.

This is a time for compassion. Religion, heritage, culture, language differences cannot divide us. The Red Cross requests that community members express their feelings about this tragedy in ways that respect all humanity, regardless of how people look, speak, or worship. We condemn all acts of violence, terror, or discrimination and appeal to everyone in our country to join in our humanitarian efforts during this time of great national emergency. America will heal, and we will be stronger.

Dana Moore

Bringing Light into the Darkness

I shall pass through this world but once. Any good that I can do or any kindness that I can show to any human being, let me do it now. Let me not defer or neglect it, for I shall not pass this way again.

—Mahatma Gandhi

September 11, 2001 changed us forever. Images fill our minds, hearts, and souls—planes crashing into the World Trade Center, the Pentagon, and the fields of Pennsylvania, towers crashing down in

Manhattan, thousands of innocent people buried in the rubble . . . tears shed . . . courageous firefighters, thousands donating blood, millions of dollars donated to relief funds, prayer and candle vigils, e-mails of comfort circulating around the world, hands held . . . tears shed . . . our own attempts to reach out to complete strangers, and pull and pull closer to loved ones, even if they were thousands of miles away, saying "I love you" over and over again.

Words cannot express the deep feelings of sadness we feel knowing so many precious lives are lost. Nor are words enough to convey the feelings of despair we are experiencing as we realize that human beings can be filled with so much hate. We wonder how we can ever make sense of the lives lost, the devastation, and the power of hate. Can we ever trust again? Are we to live in fear? Can we get to a place where the horrific images and imaginings of more to come aren't the last things we think about before falling asleep?

We may not be able to find the words to explain the unexplainable, but we can remember and honor the words and deeds of thousands of people—the passengers on the airplanes, our firefighters, rescue workers, police, medics, the victims' loved ones, strangers—who not only have brought light into such darkness, but have found ways to shine *because* of the darkness. It is in the spirit of that honoring that this book has been created.

In these pages, you'll meet folks like William Harvey, an undergraduate at Julliard who, offering the only thing he could at the time—his music—brought not only a little comfort to rescue workers, but new awareness to his own life. You'll read the story of Larry Hawk, head of the ASPCA, who put aside his own grief over his sister's death in the attacks to spearhead a movement to rescue abandoned pets at Ground Zero in New York. You'll meet Omar Tisdell, an American of Palestinian descent, who is searching for a nonviolent solution to the cycle of hate. And flight attendant Cindy Bahnij, who found a special way to honor her friends who lost their lives in the crashes. There's also the story of New York firefighter Kirk Pritchard, who, despite having a fractured spine, continued searching for his trapped brothers and sisters. Some special kids are here, too, like Annie Wignall, an enterprising thirteen-year-old who at age eleven started a nonprofit that gives personal care essentials—soap, shampoo, toothbrushes—to kids in need. When she heard of the events of September 11, she found a way to expand her delivery network to include the children of victims.

Ultimately, it is these heroes and many others whose stories must be told, retold, and cherished. For it is these people who reflect the true spirit of humanity through unconditional love. It is these people who give us hope and empower us to move past numbing fear and to take positive action. It is through their selfless example that we can find our own courage to give. And that, I believe, is the key, for it is in giving to others that we will find the healing we all are seeking.

It's not enough to read these stories and admire these folks' heroic actions. Each would tell you they don't consider themselves a hero, only an ordinary person like you or me doing what he or she could to help. They serve as role models for each of us, inspiring us to find our own courage to take action.

For some, the courage to give means donating money to a relief fund even when there aren't extra funds to give. Like the woman who signed over her unemployment check and the children who have emptied their piggy banks. For others, it's organizing a fundraiser and getting others to help raise money, like the teenage girls in Virginia who started *Wash America,* washing cars to raise money. For some it's hands-on help, like the people who drove hundreds of miles to help at Ground Zero. Or the New Yorkers who offered their services for free, such as Caren Messing, a massage therapist you'll meet in this book, who gave rescue workers massages during their breaks, and Texans who brought thousands of pounds of barbecue to serve the workers.

Those people whose giving style is hands-on may be feeling frustrated right now. We've been told no more volunteers are needed at Ground Zero. May I suggest that it is the perfect time to think about your own community? Babies still need rocking, at-risk teens still crave mentors, tutors are still needed in schools, seniors still want companionship, those in hospice care still require our love. The needs go on and on. Call your local volunteer centers and offer to help. Or check out the volunteer Web sites in the Resource Guide at the back of this book. All you have to do is get on the Internet, type in your zip code and interests, and you'll find volunteer opportunities within ten minutes of your home.

For others, finding our courage to give is about brainstorming other ways to help, creating models for making a difference, and offering suggestions to those who can make them happen. This last giving style happens to be mine. For the first forty-eight hours following the tragedy, I was numb, my heart filled with sadness, fear, and anger. Suddenly, I recognized what I was experiencing as no different than when I was diagnosed with multiple sclerosis in 1991. But now, it was our world that was diagnosed with a threatening disease. I knew from my battle with MS that only when I began helping others did my own healing begin. This situation was no different.

Realizing this, I had a vision of a book that honored our unsung heroes who put their own pain aside long enough to reach out and help another person and discovered the beginning of their own healing in the process. I would donate my royalties to the American Red Cross and the New York Firefighters 9-11 Disaster Relief Fund. The book would recount some of the miracles that occurred at a time of urgent need—thousands lining up to donate blood, friends and neighbors filling trucks with medical goods, clothes, and other supplies, people lighting candles, sending prayers and money—and ultimately this book would motivate each of us to act. I immediately called my agent, Jim Levine, and my publisher, Conari Press, and they both shouted, "Yes!" I also recognized I needed lots of help, and called upon

Brenda Welchlin, an accomplished writer, and Karen Frost, my publicist and "Finding Your Courage to Give" workshop speaker and facilitator, to donate their talents to the project. Again, another resounding "Yes!" *America, September 11: The Courage to Give* was born. Since then, everyone involved in this process—from my collaborators, agent, and publisher to the distributor and printer—have agreed to forgo all profits so that the maximum amount can be donated to these worthy causes.

We have seen buildings fall, but spirits rise. This is our monumental chance to rise to the occasion, like phoenixes out of the still-smoldering ash, to give new life to compassion and create new lives for ourselves as people who help other people. May the compelling stories you're about to read, the compassionate people you're about to meet, be a source of comfort, inspiration, and healing. May they motivate us never to forget September 11, 2001, and to choose to be changed by love, not fear. May we find our own courage to give so we may understand that true peace begins within each of us.

CHAPTER 1

Engine 1

Ladder 24

"Forever in our Hearts!"

Mike Weinberg
Engine 1
1/19/67 – 9/11/2001

KEEP BACK 500 FEET

Milwaukee Journal Sentinel by Mark Hoffman

KINDNESS AT GROUND ZERO

Jessica McBride, *Milwaukee Journal Sentinel*

*T*he clothes I wore around Ground Zero last week are piled in a corner of my hotel room, crowned by the hospital mask I breathed through for days. They stink of smoke and death. So did I, until I took two showers.

As a former police reporter, I am more inured to tragedy than most people. I have been to my share of murder scenes. This is different. The trauma here comes in waves.

On the way to New York, I passed electronic highway signs stating that New York was closed. The whole city. Closed. Who would believe that New York could be closed with the abruptness of a school during a snow emergency?

As I drove on, I thought of Lt. David Chong. Chong is a New York police lieutenant who was a keynote speaker at a Midwest gang conference two weeks ago in Milwaukee. I spoke to him for just a half-hour, but he is one of those dramatic personalities who make an impression even in the briefest of meetings.

It was devastating to imagine someone so vibrant losing his life this way. For three years, he had risked everything posing undercover as an Asian gang member. He received countless death threats. But he made it through.

Now I wondered whether he was still alive. The officials who brought him to Milwaukee—the Great Lakes International Gang Investigators Coalition—were wondering the same thing. It later turned out he had been hospitalized with a concussion. But I wonder: How many David Chongs were among the victims?

In New York, I made it past three sets of barricades and approached Ground Zero. The smoke and silt covered everything—cars, streets, people—

in a ghostly blanket. The burned hulls of squad cars were abandoned on virtually every corner. Charred papers or soda cups remained inside some of them, images of lives interrupted.

Emergency vehicles zigzagged everywhere, dodging soldiers and rescuers who were trudging around with frozen faces. The smoke chapped my lips and gave me a lingering cough.

Ground Zero was a looming mishmash of mountainous rubble. There are thousands of people in there, I kept reminding myself. Thousands of people who just vanished, turned to dust.

A friend asked if I took pictures of the area around Ground Zero.

Would you take a picture of hell?

When I walked into a firehouse, another stranger in the haze, the exhausted firefighters, just back from digging at the World Trade Center site, offered me food. I can't possibly take your food, I told them. They insisted. I refused. After the fifth firefighter offered me food, I gave in.

Firefighters are used to helping people, not being helped. The latter makes them uncomfortable. They invited me to spend the night at the firehouse, watching their rescue efforts and hearing their stories. Firefighter Jamal Braithwaite dragged a mattress into a room for me and made a comfortable bed, without being asked. Everyone takes care of everyone in Ground Zero.

The following morning, a newspaper report said a child's hand was found clutching a doll. A man and woman were found still holding hands, their wedding rings intact. The woman's head and the man's legs were missing.

As I read the newspaper in the firehouse, the emotions I had been holding back started to surge in my chest, threatening to overtake me. Firefighter Rick Saracelli was watching. He was feeling it, too. We forced the emotions down together. The brief connection helped.

As I left the firehouse in the pouring rain, a firefighter came rushing over with a pair of donated hiking boots to replace my running shoes. I can't take those, I insisted. He said they were too small for any firefighter's feet and motioned over to the mountain of donated goods they would not be able to use. Strangers had given them everything from toothbrushes to contact lens solution to T-shirts five times too small.

I took the boots, mostly to pacify him, and then set them down in a corner of the kitchen. A few minutes later, he spied the boots and asked why I wasn't wearing them. He looked hurt, so I finally put them on. They gave me a plastic rain poncho, too.

The Salvation Army, serving reporters and rescuers alike, gave me a warm cup of coffee and a pair of orange slickers not far from the station. A block later, a teenage boy offered bottled water. I took one; he said to take two. I stopped to speak with a pair of firefighters from Rhode Island whom I had met the day before, and as I was leaving, one of them shoved a pair of gloves into my hands. He didn't want my hands to get cold. I hadn't mentioned being cold. He gave me a flashlight, too.

As a reporter, I am used to being treated with animosity or aloofness at crime scenes. But everyone was in this together.

I looked down and smiled. Just about everything I was wearing had been given to me by a series of strangers. Without them, I would have been soaking wet and very cold.

After about 48 hours with minimal sleep, I needed to get someplace where gray dust wouldn't eat at my lungs and people weren't talking about picking up pieces of other people's heads. I had $6 in my pocket but needed to walk almost 50 blocks on almost no sleep to get to my hotel.

A state trooper guarding an intersection stopped me, asked me if I wanted some coffee. I thanked him.

Not far away, restaurants like Olive Garden and Hard Rock Cafe had closed to the public, and were serving rescuers for free.

Another few blocks and I was stopped by two young women who peppered me with questions. How could they help? They had heard there were no more volunteers needed because there are so many offering their services.

I imagined the firefighters heading back out to dig, covered with gray dust, talking about body parts. What could the two do? I told them to wait a week and then go down to Ground Zero and help the firefighters.

Exhausted from sleeplessness and emotion, I hailed a cab. I only have $6, I told the driver. Please take me as close to my hotel as that will get me. He took me all the way there. If the fare goes over, the New York cabbie said, don't worry about it.

Everyone is taking care of everyone now.

The New York Fire Department's Engine 54 sent fifteen men to the first call for help. None returned. The forty-five fire fighters left behind worked 24-hour shifts and returned to the attack site on their own time to search for their comrades. While they were gone, folks in the neighborhood built a tribute—with food donations, flowers, cards, candles, American flags under the photos of the station's missing firefighters.

CHAPTER 2

Ira Rosenblum

PLAYING FOR THE FIGHTING 69TH

William Harvey

*O*n September 16, 2001, I had the most incredible and moving experience of my life. Juilliard organized a quartet to play at the Armory in New York. The Armory is a huge military building where families of people missing from the disaster went to wait for news of their loved ones. Entering the building was very difficult emotionally, because the entire building, the size of a city block, was completely covered with posters of missing people. Thousands of posters, spread out up to eight feet above the ground, each featuring a different, smiling, face.

I made my way to the huge central room and found my Juilliard buddies. For two hours the three of us sight-read quartets. I don't think I will soon forget the grief counselor from the Connecticut State Police who listened the entire time, or the woman who listened only to "Memories" from *Cats,* crying the whole time.

At 7 P.M., the other two players had to leave; they had been playing at the Armory since one in the afternoon and simply couldn't play any more. I volunteered to stay and play solo, since I had just gotten there.

I soon realized that the evening had just begun for me: a man in fatigues who introduced himself as Sergeant Major asked me if I'd mind playing for his soldiers as they came back from digging through the rubble at Ground Zero. Masseuses had volunteered to give his men massages, he said, and he didn't think anything would be more soothing than getting a massage and listening to violin music at the same time. So at 9 P.M., I headed up to the second floor where the soldiers were arriving. From then until 11:30 P.M., I played everything I could from memory: Bach *B Minor Partita,* Tchaikovsky *Concerto,* Dvorak *Concerto,* Paganini *Caprices* 1 and 17, Vivaldi *Winter* and *Spring,* the theme from *Schindler's List,* Tchaikovsky *Melodie, Meditation from*

Thais, "Amazing Grace," "My Country 'Tis of Thee," "Turkey in the Straw," "Boil Dem Cabbage Down."

Never have I played for a more grateful audience. Somehow it didn't matter that by the end, my intonation was shot and I had no bow control. I would have lost any competition I was playing in, but it didn't matter. The men would come up the stairs in full gear, remove their helmets, look at me, and smile.

At 11:20 P.M., I was introduced to Col. Slack, head of the regiment. After thanking me, he said to his friends, "Boy, today was the toughest day yet. I made the mistake of going back into the pit, and I'll never do that again."

Eager to hear a first-hand account, I asked, "What did you see?" He stopped, swallowed hard, and said, "What you'd expect to see." The colonel stood there as I played a lengthy rendition of "Amazing Grace," which he claimed was the best he'd ever heard. By this time it was 11:30 P.M., and I didn't think I could play anymore. I asked Sergeant Major if it would be appropriate if I played the National Anthem. He shouted above the chaos of the milling soldiers to call them to attention, and I played as the men of the 69th Regiment saluted an invisible flag.

After shaking a few hands and packing up, I was leaving when one of the privates accosted me to say that the colonel wanted to see me again. He took me down to the War Room, but we couldn't find the colonel, so he gave me a tour of the War Room.

It turns out that the regiment I played for is the Famous Fighting 69th, the most decorated regiment in the U.S. Army. He pointed out a letter the division received from Abraham Lincoln, offering his condolences after the Battle of Antietam—the 69th suffered the most casualties of any division at that historic battle. Finally, we located the colonel. After thanking me again, he presented me with the coin of the regiment. "We only give these to someone who's done something special for the 69th," he informed me. He called over the regiment's historian to tell me the significance of all the symbols on the coin.

As I rode the taxi back to Juilliard—free, of course, since taxi service was free in New York during this time—I was numb. Not only was this evening the proudest I've ever felt to be an American, it was my most meaningful as a musician and a person. At Juilliard, kids can be critical of each other and competitive. Teachers expect, and in many cases get, technical perfection. But this wasn't about that. The soldiers didn't care that I had so many memory slips I lost count. They didn't care that when I forgot how the second movement of the Tchaikovsky went, I had to come up with my own improvisation until I somehow got to a cadence. I've never seen a more appreciative audience, and I've never understood so fully what it means to communicate music to other people.

And how did it change me as a person? Let's just say that next time I want to get into a petty argument about whether Richter or Horowitz was better, I'll remember that when I asked the colonel to describe the pit formed by the tumbling of the Towers, he couldn't. Words only go so far, and even music can only go a little further from there.

> When planes were grounded, the American Red Cross teamed up with Amtrak and Coca-Cola to establish the Clara Barton Express train to bring essential supplies into New York City. The train, named after the founder of the American Red Cross, was used to transport 20,000 cleanup kits, 20,000 hygiene kits, cases of paper tissues and beverages. Included in the supplies were eye drops and dust masks, two items not normally delivered to disaster scenes.

CHAPTER 3

AP/Wide World Photos

WITH COMPASSION AND BRAVERY

*B*right Horizons Family Solutions is the world's leading provider of employer-sponsored child care, early education, and work/life consulting services, managing more than 365 child care and early education centers in the United States, Europe, and the Pacific Rim. Bright Horizons serves more than 300 clients, including eighty-one Fortune 500 companies and forty-four of the "100 Best Companies for Working Mothers," as recognized by *Working Mother* magazine. Bright Horizons was recently named one of the "100 Best Companies to Work for in America" by *Fortune* magazine. One of their childcare centers was just around the corner from the World Trade Center. What follows is an excerpt of a letter the Chairman of the Board wrote recently to her staff.

To the Bright Horizons community,

I have just returned from New York City where we are launching, in partnership with J. P MorganChase and Mercy Corps, an emergency response effort on behalf of children and families. We have an excellent, highly skilled team and we have already moved into high gear. We will be providing a variety of services and materials for children, parents, and caregivers. Please check our website (www.brighthorizons.com) for further information and details on how to help.

Traveling around NY was a shock. I drove into the city late Sunday night. I saw the familiar skyline with the Chrysler building, the Empire State building, and others all lit up. But of course, the view of lower Manhattan was shocking with the absence of the World Trade Center towers. Lower Manhattan was lit brightly by floodlights as emergency crews worked around the clock. Smoke still billows skyward.

I have worked and lived in a variety of disaster spots around the world. The environment now in NYC felt all too familiar to me, although I never thought I would feel this way in my own country. We have long been sheltered from the terror that other cultures live with around the world. Police were everywhere, streets were blocked off, security in all buildings was tight. Everywhere you walked you saw posters plastered on walls of loved ones lost. People are afraid and somber.

One of our centers is a few short blocks from the World Trade Center. Joan Cesaretti, Haifa Bautista, and the faculty showed tremendous compassion and bravery during the crisis. As the towers crumbled, scores of panicked people escaping the towers stampeded into the center, covered in inches of ash and dust. The teachers and directors responded and ministered to all who came in. They washed and bandaged cuts, they washed eyes and faces, they ripped up crib sheets to make face masks as the area rapidly became thick with smoke. They talked to panicked victims and kept them calm. Only one child was left in the center, and teacher Ingrid Gutierrez refused to put her down for hours until they could find the child's mother. At one point a fireman rushed into the center and urgently ordered them to evacuate immediately. As they stepped outside, the child looked around and said, "What happened to the world?" None of us know the answer.

Fortunately, all parents and children were accounted for, and no one was lost and injured from our community. Our other NYC centers became a sanctuary for children and parents. In one center, families stayed in the center for most of the day with their children.

They felt safe, protected, and nurtured in the childcare center environment. They had no idea how they would get home. Teachers kept the children engaged and busy, and the children's spirits helped everyone to be strong.

Linda Mason, Chairman of the Board, Co-Founder, Bright Horizons Family Solutions

The day of the attack, ferries, tugboats, and dinghies appeared on the banks of Manhattan to bring people to safety.

A TASTE OF LOVE, TEXAS–STYLE

Jennifer Emily, *Dallas Morning News*

$\mathcal{W}$ ith 1,000 pounds of brisket, 800 pounds of ranch-style beans and shirts proclaiming "Texas ♥ New York," a group of DeSoto volunteers began feeding rescue workers this weekend to show their support for them and the nation.

Sixteen men, many of them truck drivers, from Rhema Ranch Ministries came in six refrigerated semis and a bus to help workers who are searching for the more than 6,000 people missing in the rubble of the World Trade Center.

"I came with a giving heart," Rhema Ranch volunteer Scott Jackson said as he waited for the food to cook. "I wanted to be a blessing, as these . . . [rescue workers] are a blessing. As we all watched the situation unfold, we knew we had to help. It's just too close to home."

The grill has been loaded with food nonstop since the DeSoto volunteers arrival Friday night. The men sleep in shifts—like the rescue workers they serve—so food is always available. They have served hundreds of people, including police, firefighters and other volunteers.

Chris Beauvais, an ironworker from Quebec, said the wood-smoked barbecue was a welcome addition to the meals other volunteers serve.

"We stop here every day. The Texas boys just got here," he said, pointing a fork full of ranch-style beans in their direction. "Now that's barbecue."

Mr. Beauvais has been working an eight-hour shift each day since Sept. 13, carefully cutting through the rubble of the trade center. He was working on top of a building at New York University when he saw the two planes crash into the World Trade Center.

The DeSoto volunteers set up their grill outside the Jacob K. Javits Convention Center, where the rescue workers sleep. In addition to the New York

City police, firefighters and ironworkers, about 500 volunteers from the Federal Emergency Management Agency are helping with the rescue efforts.

More Than Just Food

Jacques Parrish, another DeSoto volunteer, said he was not prepared for the extent of the devastation. He said he offers the food, a smile and a kind word to help the rescue workers cope.

"It's hard for them to handle," he said.

Most of the people supplying food to the rescue workers are distributing prepackaged meals such as sandwiches. Only one other person besides the Rhema Ranch volunteers is distributing hot meals near the convention center.

"I Love My Country"

Ron Riviezzo, a chef from Key West, Fla., took time off from work to prepare pasta, bean soup and casseroles for the workers.

He had been visiting his sister in New Jersey when the planes crashed into the trade center.

"I love my country," he said, explaining why he took time off from his job.

Workers also can pick up cough medicine, eye drops, toothpaste and other medicines and hygiene products.

Many of the volunteers are not as well-organized as the Rhema Ranch group, which also provides substance-abuse counseling in Texas.

Erik Esquerra of San Francisco drove to New York to provide assistance after the trade center collapsed.

He began by collecting and distributing supplies such as masks and gloves. When officials told him to go home because they had more than enough volunteers, he began helping various groups distribute food.

"I just wanted to help; this is how I could do it," he said.

David Nunez, a Phoenix firefighter and Arizona Task Force-1 member for FEMA, said, "The people here have been real good to us."

Mr. Nunez, who was preparing for a 7 P.M.-to-7 A.M. shift at the trade center, ate a plate of spaghetti before moving on to the brisket.

"Tasty," he said after finishing it. "It's good to have a hot meal."

A seventeen-year-old boy who lost his father four years ago and feels for the suffering of the children involved wanted to make a difference. When he found out he was too young to give blood, he donated his allowance to the Red Cross.

LABOR OF LOVE

Tonya Maxwell, *Asheville Citizen-Times*

*M*eal plans and personal hygiene kit preparations crowd Bethany Putnam's thoughts. But at the moment, her priority is instructing people to move supplies that are across the street from a looming black building. It is Building 5 of the World Trade Center complex. On Sunday, inspectors feared it might fall. The supplies had to be moved. "If people want to continue using this stuff, that's great," Putnam tells a volunteer beneath a makeshift tent assembled from blue tarps. "But I'm not comfortable with people being down here."

"Down here" is on a street corner behind St. Paul's Chapel, the oldest church in Manhattan. It is the church of George Washington, a block away from rubble that was the south tower of the World Trade Center. Putman, an Asheville, North Carolina, resident, helps people who help people. Through the nonprofit group she started, Labor of Love, Putnam makes sure volunteers and rescue workers have food, foot care, and toothbrushes. She makes sure they have organization. Putnam began Labor of Love more than two years ago after tornadoes swept Oklahoma City. She took a group of eleven people to help with relief efforts there.

Then a chef and caterer in Michigan, Putnam saw a need in the Episcopalian church for a volunteer coordinator capable of working on large sites. Since then, she has left her job, moved to Asheville, and more fully developed Labor of Love with assistance from the Cathedral of All Souls. Often disaster sites need help months, even years, after time has eroded media concern and the empathy of outsiders. Putman prefers to go to an area after the initial salve and bandages have worn away. But when an official from the Episcopalian Trinity Parish on Wall Street in New York called to ask for Putnam's help, she packed a bag.

But before she left, she called Katherine Avery, a twenty-four-year-old from Spartanburg, South Carolina. Avery had interviewed for a job with Labor of Love the Friday before the planes were hijacked. Putnam called to tell Avery she was hired. "She said, 'Sit down,'" Avery recalled with a smile. "She told me I had the job and then she said she was going to New York and wanted to know if I was available to go." She was. Putnam also told Avery she couldn't pay her, not right yet. Labor of Love has never known the luxury of a budget. At the moment, it's not a detail that concerns Avery. It'll work out, she believes.

Now, with Avery's help, Putnam coordinates the twenty or so volunteers who come through St. Paul's Chapel each hour. They focus a fleet of volunteer hands on chores that help oil the rescue machine. When Putnam arrived on the Friday, that meant reorganizing supplies so workers could find paper towels and toilet paper with ease. Saturday, that meant sending volunteers to wash the twenty loads of linens so firefighters and police would have clean sheets as they sprawl out on pews. Sunday night, that meant locating cans of coffee; the supply threatened to run out before morning.

In terms of volunteer needs, the World Trade Center disaster is little different than the four other sites Putnam has coordinated, she said. Except, of course, the obvious. The sheer magnitude of its scale. That scale demands more volunteers, more supplies. Boxes of mouthwash, socks, disposable razors, and a dozen other necessities line the walls of St. Paul's Chapel. They push against a cubicle-sized area that demarcates the pew of the nation's first president.

Inside the partitioned area where Washington once worshiped, a podiatrist has a makeshift station. She offers quick foot care to rescuers who have spent many of the last days crammed in work boots. All of this at St. Paul's Chapel, a haven at the edge of Ground Zero, is Putnam's responsibility. It's just a matter of being hospitable, she said.

"It's challenging to access the needs of not only a community, but also of the volunteers coming in with their own visions of how to help," Putnam said. "There is always a disaster. There are always people that want to help. It's a matter of bringing them together."

A group called Squares That Care in Fort Mill, South Carolina, created three red, white, and blue quilts from squares donated by individuals from around the country, complete with the names and cities of the donors. They will be given at Christmas in memory of the victims of the three crash sites.

CHAPTER 6

AP/Wide World Photos

Washing Away the Hurt

From *redcross.org*

*F*ollowing the September 11 attacks, four girls from Annandale, Virginia—Ashley, Aubrey, Alana, and Alyssa Welch—went with their mother to donate blood. They wanted to contribute to the relief efforts because their father, Lt. Col. Tracy Welch, narrowly escaped the Pentagon crash.

Their father, who had a meeting scheduled that morning in the west wing of the Pentagon, was in Crystal City and about to leave for the meeting when the plane struck. "He was supposed to be there," said Alana, fourteen. "But it was like he was destined to be okay."

Relieved that their father was unhurt, the girls were concerned for those who weren't as fortunate and wanted to help in some way. Aged ten to sixteen, the girls are too young to give blood, but a friend suggested a car wash. The girls grabbed hold of the idea, and even took it a step further, organizing four local car wash events that raised $10,000. They made and distributed fliers, designed posters, and contacted local media to help spread the word.

Now their efforts have gained steam and expanded to the national level. The girls have launched a national car wash campaign—Wash America: Help Wash Away the Hurt—to give kids across the country an outlet for their sense of loss and their urge to help. Wash America asks kids around the United States to sponsor weekend car washes—starting this weekend—to raise money for the American Red Cross.

"People from all over are asking us how they can help," said Ashley, sixteen. "The support has been incredible."

Kids who want to sponsor Wash America car washes in their communities can log on to the Wash America Web site at www.washamerica.org. The site includes tips and checklists for organizing a car wash, as well as information on how to send money to the designated account for Red Cross relief efforts.

In response to the terrorist attacks, a former Cuban refugee, Raquel Dominguez, helped sew 10,000 American flags at Freedom Flags of Miami. A boat person picked up by the Coast Guard, she said that when rescued, the American flag was the most beautiful thing she had ever seen, so sewing the flag was a contribution that was easy to make.

Teachers on the Front Lines

Sue Shellenbarger, *Wall Street Journal*

*I*s worksite child care safe? Amid new fears for children, many parents wonder whether bringing kids to high-profile, visible workplaces is unwise. Among all the tales of Sept. 11 heroism are two stories that should reassure parents: How teachers at the World Trade Center and Pentagon child-care centers safely evacuated the children in their charge.

The fourteen teachers at Children's Discovery Center in 5 World Trade Center, a building that later partly collapsed, had taken in only 42 early arrivals by the time the first plane hit that morning.

As the ground shook, teachers grabbed each child's emergency records, took babies in their arms and, following a drill they practiced every month, led the children outside, leaving behind their own purses and, in some cases, their own shoes, says Kristin Thomas, head of northeast operations for Knowledge Learning, the San Rafael, Calif., operator of the center. Some parents raced in to pick up children, too, leaving staffers with just 28 kids.

Once outside, the ragtag band was barred by police from the preset evacuation destination, 7 World Trade. Then, the second plane hit. Split into two groups by flying debris and hordes of fleeing people, teachers began walking north. One group picked up several shopping carts from a grocery store and helped toddlers inside, telling them, "We're going for a little ride," Ms. Thomas says. Some passing businessmen tore off their white shirts to cover the children.

Some teachers, with babies propped on their hips, were soon barefoot; the paper booties they'd donned in the center's infant room had shredded from all the walking. Armed with the emergency records, staffers borrowed phones to get messages to parents. Both groups trekked more than a mile before coming to rest, one in a hospital and the second in a preschool. All the kids were returned safe to parents; in the preschool, many were napping on cots as parents arrived.

At the Pentagon, Shirley Allen, director of the Children's World Learning Center, had plenty to worry about after Flight 77 plowed into the building. Her husband, a naval officer, worked in an office directly in the path. But Ms. Allen, a 12-year child-care veteran, thought only of evacuating the 148 children in her center, located about 30 yards from the Pentagon. In a process also honed by monthly drills, she and her 36 staffers rounded up youngsters, put babies in mobile cribs and set out across a park.

Hundreds of panicky workers ran past the children. Rescue workers relocated Ms. Allen's group five times. Again and again, she had to demand loudly that security officers accompany the kids as they moved. Heart pounding, she fought fears that a child would be lost.

But with the children, she and the teachers, many of them equally experienced, kept calm. "The children were relaxed, because they looked into their teachers' faces and saw they were relaxed," Ms. Allen says. To distract them, teachers played pat-a-cake and sang "Eensy Weensy Spider." Not until three hours later, with the children safe and most of them back in parents' care, did Ms. Allen allow herself to think of her husband. She burst into tears. Two hours later, she finally learned he was safe. Three children at the center, Ms. Allen says, her voice breaking, lost a parent. The center re-opened Monday.

Child-care teachers generally aren't paid enough to reflect the awesome responsibilities they bear. Both the Pentagon and the World Trade child-care centers were high-quality facilities subsidized by employers. That support helped produce the policies, training and employee-retention programs that prepared these staffers so well. Bright Horizons Family Solutions, a high-quality child-care concern, won't even open a worksite facility without employer support, in subsidies or facilities.

Operations chiefs at several big child-care chains say they'll study government or military locations more carefully before opening new centers, but none said they plan to pull back. Joseph Silverman, president of Day Care Insurance Services, an Encino, Calif., brokerage, says exits should be safe and accessible, and centers probably shouldn't be above the second floor.

That said, worksite child care is still one of the safest places to leave a child. "Do I keep a day-care facility out of the Pentagon? Probably not," Mr. Silverman says. "You start thinking that way: Do I keep a day-care facility off an earthquake fault line? Do I keep a day-care facility off a flight path? And where do you stop?" Roughly three million children attend child-care centers safely every day.

In dangerous times, parents want their kids near them. Child-care center enrollments haven't fallen in Oklahoma City since the 1995 attack on the federal building there, a blast that killed 19 kids in a center. Centers in U.S. government buildings have since grown about 10%.

Perhaps parents' biggest job is banishing fear—putting on a calm face, as these teachers did, so children can stay calm. "Children, of course, always have giants and monsters in their minds, but now the adults do, too," says Bright Horizons' Jim Greenman. "At some level, we have to remember: We know how to cope with this."

In tribute to all those who died in the attacks, on September 14 at noon in Switzerland, all traffic, even the ever-punctual trains, stopped. People stood in silence amid churchbells ringing and prayed for America and the victims.

CHAPTER 8

Larry   Kim   Kathy   Jim

Jennifer Hawk

BEYOND THE SELF

*L*arry Hawk finished his morning e-mail to his teenagers in Arizona just minutes before the plane his sister was traveling on struck the World Trade Center. It was a daily ritual for the divorced dad, the typical "not much news here, but I love you."

The president of the American Society for the Prevention of Cruelty to Animals (ASPCA) had been in his office on Manhattan's Upper East Side, immersed in budgets, capital campaigns, and plans for a new building. Filming was wrapping up for an episode of *Animal Precinct,* an Animal Planet show that chronicles the work of animal rescue workers in New York City. Once people in the office began hearing news of a flaming tower, a plane crash, they quickly shifted their focus to television sets and news reports.

A private pilot himself, Larry knew that flying carried risks, but he did not track his Boston-based flight attendant sister's flight schedules. "I didn't know my sister was on that particular flight, but I knew she always flew the west coast flights. And I just hoped she wasn't flying that day."

ASPCA management tried to convene a "What do we do from here?" meeting sometime between the first plane's impact and the first tower's collapse. "It was probably shortly after that second tower collapsed that I received a call from my mother. She told me it had been my sister's flight."

Kathy Nicosia, fifty-four, had flown for more than three decades. Besides her mother, two brothers and a sister, she left behind a husband and a college-age daughter.

"That was a pretty tough phone call to take. I was at the office and really didn't have a lot of time to fully grieve. I had to deal with what was happening here. We had a lot of employees who had loved ones or friends at or near the World Trade Center."

Hawk told a few senior managers about his mother's call but otherwise turned his attention to his employees. "I wasn't really ready to share it. There were a lot of other people to be concerned about."

Eventually, the office shut down, and workers left to tend to their families and friends. "For myself, that meant beginning to deal with the reality that I'd lost my big sister," Larry said. "I think a lot of people are dealing with post-traumatic stress, visions, things in the middle of the night. I'm grappling with it all. I've had to come to the conclusion that I have to really look at it that lives weren't lost in vain. Yes, it was 7,000 people. My sister was one of them. But I can't believe it was in vain. It woke up a sleeping nation. And hopefully that loss will prevent much worse in the future. I have to maintain that belief."

Within a few days, as he shared his story with more people, it became clear that the ASPCA would have a vital role to play in responding to the destruction. "That's part of what kept me going. We knew we had a job to do, and we knew what we had to do."

A hotline number was posted immediately. The agency's usual 10,000 weekly calls grew to 10,000 daily. A street-by-street, building-by-building database of animal needs was assembled. The ASPCA is normally linked with the New York office of the Federal Emergency Management Agency, but that link had been severed with the destruction of one of the buildings. Hawk waited for the city's assessment of its needs as they related to animals, but that assessment never came.

"Finally we made the determination that we just had to assemble a crew and go down there. We'd take our medical unit; we'd take our humane law enforcement officers; we would go with our vehicles and just assess what in fact the situation was, what we could do, how we could aid and not make this tragedy any worse."

The ASPCA sent humane law enforcement officers—peace officers trained to work with animals—to escort residents, one by one, back home to retrieve their pets. They found great cooperation among the New York Police Department and National Guard members who were stationed at the barricades. "We wouldn't have been able to do that without that cooperative effort between those agencies, and sometimes it was the person at the barricade taking trust and faith in our uniformed officers, saying, 'Okay, this is a fellow uniformed peace officer, and I'm going to allow them to pass,'" Larry said. "That cooperative effort, despite the chaos and confusion, was a real strong point."

The ASPCA helped rescue 200 pets, and treated more than 300 at medical command centers, mostly for dehydration. Only one pet was lost in the process—a cat with kidney disease that died shortly after being rescued.

"One ASPCA officer went with a teenager who had a gecko on the 38th floor. The teenager didn't make it up all thirty-eight floors, but he did," Hawk said. The ASPCA rescued cats, dogs, bunnies, turtles, hamsters, fish— "all sort of sundry pets."

Larry Hawk was asked repeatedly by reporters how he could focus on animals at a time of such great human devastation. The focus, he said, was squarely on people initially, as it should have been. But the ASPCA also recognizes the importance of animals in people's lives—as family members and as sources of comfort.

"When these people were reunited with their pets, it was just an incredible feeling to watch. They had been so panicked, and they were so filled with joy and glee that they had their pet back. One man said to my team, 'I can't thank you enough for reuniting me with my four-legged family. It means so much to me,' he said, 'because here's a picture of my wife. Here are some of my leaflets. Would you help me put them around? She's still missing.' Here's a man whose wife was missing but had his cat back and even offered to take an orphan cat that we had at the time."

As part of the ASPCA team, Larry traveled to Lower Manhattan. "I was able to get down and see probably more than I should have. It was a bit surreal being here in New York, where it happened, working with my staff and others. In a way it was good because I was able to help, and I did get a lot of support from my coworkers, from other total strangers that came up to me at our command centers, and it was very heartwarming to experience that. From that standpoint, it was good to be here. At the same time, it added sights, sounds, smells which were all very, very real to an already horrible situation. I'm maybe dealing with things that my other family members haven't had to. I can smell the smoke; I saw the smoke; I was near the scene. It just got that much more up-close and personal for me."

But for the most part, he tried to stay away from the destruction, to give his employees room to work. "I tried to stay away from them, let them do their job. We wanted to be able to do our job well. And it wasn't about me; it wasn't about my sister. This was about helping people with their pets and getting them reunited."

And it was about unity on a larger scale, as well, he said. "If you look at what's happened—how New Yorkers came together, how my team at the ASPCA came together, how the nation has jelled, come together, how the world is starting to unite—I think it's great to see.

"I hope we have the courage to sustain that, the fortitude to sustain that."

A man from Germany called the Red Cross phone bank. He wanted to send his entire EMT unit all the way to Washington or New York, wherever they were needed most. Said the volunteer who took the call, "I can't tell you how moving it was to hear him trying desperately to find a way to help. Without a doubt, the people calling the hotline are willing to do anything to help those who need them most right now."

CHAPTER 9

AP/Wide World Photos

PENTAGON HEROES

Ron Kampeas, Associated Press

*T*hey believed they were in the most secure building in the strongest country in the world. Then a hijacked plane smashed into the Pentagon, their fortress. Yet they knew just what to do.

Knocked onto his back, Army Lt. Col. Victor Correa picked himself up from the floor and helped dazed colleagues out of the room. He headed for a wall of smoke down a hall littered with ceiling tiles, illuminated only by distant flames.

His big, booming voice was a natural to lead people to safety. "I was screaming, 'Listen to me. Listen to me. Follow my voice,'" Correa recalled. "Folks started coming out."

Correa peered into the smoke, a water-soaked T-shirt pressed to his face. No one had to tell him what to do. "All of us had a different function, and I knew what mine was," he said.

All across the Pentagon, years of military training and discipline kicked in. After an unfounded warning that a second aircraft was on its way, Correa forced open fire doors that had slammed shut. He went back in and started shouting again.

His shouting drew Carl Mahnken back to consciousness. Mahnken, a civilian in the Army public affairs office, got up from the rubble-strewn floor and followed the voices through the smoke. Outside, he saw medics assisting the wounded. He ran over to help.

"You knew what to do, you ripped pants open, you took shoes off, you learned to help people with their shock, to get the blood flowing," said Mahnken, an Army reservist trained in first aid.

It was not until hours later, in the evening, that a firefighter told Mahnken about the golf-ball-sized bump protruding from his crown. That was when he remembered his computer terminal flying toward his head, hours earlier. "He gave me an ice pack," he said. "I hadn't noticed."

Army Sgt. Maj. Tony Rose heard cries for help from behind a mountain of debris inside one room and set up a tunnel-digging team, working on rotation. One particularly hefty Navy Seal propped up the sagging ceiling.

"I forget his name," Rose said. "We just called him 'Big John.'" They had helped seven people out through the impromptu tunnel when a wall buckled. They got out before it collapsed.

There was a call for volunteers in another area. "There were some walking wounded, but everyone who could turned back," Rose said. "We had no maps, no flashlights, just wet T-shirts."

Some refused even to talk about themselves, insisting on recounting the heroism they witnessed. Lt. Col. Sean Kelly singled out Army colleague Capt. Darrell Oliver. After Kelly and Oliver lifted a desk off a secretary, Oliver hoisted her onto his back and carried her out. Then he returned for a hearing impaired janitor who was sobbing in fear.

"He calmed him down, he carried him out over the partitions, over the furniture," Kelly said. Kelly also noted National Guard Lt. Col. Larry Dudney, hacking from smoke inhalation as he lifted furniture off of his colleagues.

Each man said military training was key to the disciplined response—although each hastened to note that the civilians were also cool and resourceful. "The thing with the military," Kelly said, "is that you ask for one volunteer, you get fifty—you're trained for crisis."

Rose marveled as he recalled shouting orders at generals among the volunteers bagging body parts around the wreckage. "I sort of became the old sergeant major out there," he said. "People, regardless of rank, fell in and did what was needed."

Constantly on the rescuers' minds is the thought about what was left undone: 188 people believed dead from the plane and inside the Defense Department headquarters.

"I knew I had to leave when (the smoke) got worse. I think I did the right thing," Correa said. "There are questions I'll have to live with for the rest of my life."

Some answers have already come: "I've been approached by several folks who said, 'That was the voice I heard.'"

A group of children from Arlington, Virginia, set up a lemonade stand on their street the first weekend after the attack, selling lemonade, baked goods, and dog biscuits. Many residents offered to pay a little more than the prices listed, it seems, for by Monday morning, the children showed up at the Pentagon disaster headquarters with $1,140.20 for the Red Cross.

THE SEARCH FOR SOLACE

Debra Nussbaum Cohen, *Jewish Week*

*S*tanding in the rubble of Ground Zero, Rabbi Avi Weiss found spiritual sustenance, and a new cadre of religious mentors, in a place haunted by death. Listening to the stories told by rescue workers and clergy who had come from distant points to help in the World Trade Center relief effort, "They became my rebbes," said Rabbi Weiss. "I would stand near a makeshift morgue with priests, and as they took out bodies and placed them in these refrigerated trucks, we would just hug each other. I found interacting with them extraordinarily meaningful. That was a source of more spiritual energy."

Rabbis all over the country, besieged by the faithful, were thirsting for "spiritual energy," and for wisdom, following the terror attacks in New York and Washington. And while experienced rabbis such as Avi Weiss received calls from junior rabbis on how to deal with the enormity of the tragedy, they, in turn, found consolation and solace where they could—from congregants, from family, and from God. And, in Rabbi Weiss' case, from complete strangers.

"The key in this rabbinic effort is to listen much more than to talk. One is comforted as one comforts," said Rabbi Weiss of the Hebrew Institute of Riverdale.

Rabbi Simkha Weintraub, to whom dozens of other rabbis began turning immediately after the World Trade Centers collapsed, is a man who usually has a ready, thoughtful answer to most any question. When asked who takes care of his spiritual and emotional needs, he fell silent. After a pause, he said, "It's one of the first times that I can say without embarrassment that God does."

Rabbis of every denomination sought Rabbi Weintraub's input on how to address the terror in sermons, and where to find resources to assist in counseling adults and children. They also subtly sought to process their own feelings about the catastrophe.

"Rabbis, like social workers, don't usually say, 'I need to talk about how I'm feeling,' but it's the subtext. They'll say, 'I'm shook up,'" said Rabbi Weintraub.

He has been perhaps uniquely qualified to respond to their calls and e-mail. A Conservative rabbi, he works as the rabbinic director of the National Center for Jewish Healing and its parent body, the New York Jewish Board of Family & Children's Services. He is also a certified social worker and has a small private psychotherapy practice.

But Rabbi Weintraub is not alone in providing solace and advice to colleagues. Experienced rabbis everywhere are fielding calls from others. Rabbi David Ellenson, president of the Reform movement's Hebrew Union College-Jewish Institute of Religion, is based in Los Angeles, where his family lives, but was in New York at the time tragedy struck. "Rabbis are struggling with how to give people a sense of meaning," said Rabbi Ellenson, who fielded a number of calls from colleagues. "How do you give articulate voice to the pain people feel in light of a tragedy like this? In light of the evil people are capable of committing, how do you continue to provide them with a sense of optimism and hope? That is the real challenge to rabbis right now.

"Most of my colleagues weren't looking to provide an answer to why this happened, because I'm not sure an adequate answer exists. But people wanted their rabbis to give them a language to even be able to begin to confront the tragedies that have befallen us at this moment." Rabbi Ellenson himself turned to two Los Angeles rabbis, whom he spoke with over Rosh HaShanah, by which time he had been able to rejoin his family: Reform Rabbi Sanford Ragins of Leo Baeck Temple and Conservative Rabbi Elliott Dorf of the University of Judaism. "Each was able to express the horror that all of us feel and simultaneously allowed us, in very poetic language, not to forfeit our humanity despite the terrible events of last week."

Rabbi Irving "Yitz" Greenberg, a leading Modern Orthodox thinker, doesn't have a pulpit, but students and others look to him for guidance. And the rabbi, who works as president of the Jewish Life Network, an educational foundation, and as chairman of the U.S. Holocaust Memorial Commission, has developed a theology responding to the challenge of coping spiritually with nearly inconceivable horrors. "Five people asked me just in the last few days why there is innocent suffering, because of the random and tragic nature of this," he said. "Of course there's no answer. It's not that the rabbis' rabbis have better answers than other people." But his theology of an "evolving covenant," which he developed in response to the Holocaust, also applies now. God's relationship with humankind is an evolving one, playing out in stages, according to Rabbi Greenberg. "As time goes on God intervenes less and less because it's a maturing relationship, and people have more free will. It's not a magic power that prevents things like this, but a covenantal human response. Terrorists should have been stopped before."

And so Rabbi Greenberg's response to the eternal question in the face of tragedy, "Where was God?" is to ask: "Where were we?" Asked whom he turns to for solace and guidance in times like these, Rabbi Greenberg at first laughed. And then he talked about his father, who, though now dead twenty-six years, is still missed for the comfort he provided. Now, he said, he turns to his wife, Blu, other family members, and Jewish texts. "When you turn to Talmud or to Torah or to Prophets, you're contacting the authorities of the past," he said, "and then there are living teachers, too. But neither living nor dead teachers give you definitive answers."

Twenty-three-year-old Nick Branham from Kentucky quit his job, emptied his savings account, and drove 700 miles to New York City a day after the tragedy to see how he could lend a hand. Asked why he went, he said, "I don't know nobody that died in this [but] I just kept feeling worse and worse. Every answer I got from praying was to go. It was the strongest feeling I ever had in my life. I've done a lot of wrong, and I've messed up a lot of times. But I'll never be the same person just from what I've seen. It's going to stick with me until I'm dead."

Jason Kordelos, Marian and Aidan Fontana

David Fontana

TO CARE FOR MY FRIEND

*J*ason Kordelos had planned to spend the evening with Aidan Fontana, the five-year-old son of his best friend. He would pick the child up from school so Aidan's parents, David and Marian Fontana, could celebrate their September 11 anniversary.

He arose about 10 A.M. that day, urged awake by a phone that wouldn't stop ringing. He flipped on the television; the World Trade Center was aflame. He began checking messages. Marian had called to say that David, a firefighter just coming off a 24-hour shift, had gone to the scene to help out but would be home in about an hour. The anniversary plans were still on. "She and I were going to coordinate house keys and things like that."

Jason turned back to the television. "As I saw the first tower falling, I called her right away, and she picked up the phone, pretty much screaming and crying," Jason said. "She's screaming, 'Oh, my God, he's going to be— he's dead, he's dead.' I said, 'I'll be right there.'"

Jason called his mother in San Francisco, then ran the eight blocks to Marian's home, where a few of her girlfriends had already gathered. "She's a pretty together woman, but she was falling apart—crying, screaming. I wouldn't say hysterical, but pretty close. It was a typical job of just saying, 'I'm sure he's just fine. I'm sure he's going to call. I'm sure he can't call' because at that point cell service had stopped, phone lines were already jammed."

Most of the people gathered at the house thought David wouldn't have had time to reach the towers, and they were just trying to absorb the disparate events.

"Meanwhile, Marian was trying to hope that her husband hadn't been close enough by. So then the second tower fell, and it felt like the end of the world," Jason said. "From then on it seems like it has just been a nonstop roller coaster of horror and emotion—and togetherness, as well. At that moment, everyone in the world's life changed. I certainly felt a profound change for me with her. Early on in that afternoon, after a few hours where she could kind of get her head around the horror of the possibility of her husband being dead, she said, 'You're going to have to help me raise my son if this is as bad as I think it is.' And I said, 'Of course.'"

Aidan was still at school, and arrangements were made for him to go home with a friend to spend the night. Marian talked with Aidan briefly on the phone, and he sounded like he was having fun. At the friend's house, the boys talked about going up on the roof to see the big accident.

Back at home, the clock edged forward.

That first night, alone, was the deepest and darkest. At 2 A.M., they turned out the lights, leaving a blue haze from the television, tuned to VH-1. Marian, who could not sleep in her own bed, rested on the couch, while Jason found a spot on the floor.

"People demand so much of the spouse, it seems, in this situation. She can't give it. She can't function. She can barely sit up," Jason said. "Sitting through that first night, she slept barely at all. We got some sleeping pills, but they didn't work. That was the most miserable time of my life, those few hours until daylight came, and then it was just miserable in a different way."

They learned that the truck David had ridden to the scene had been found under debris. Twelve members of his squad went to the scene initially. None returned. Two of their bodies were found in the first three weeks.

By the time Aidan came home from his friend's house the next day, Marian's parents had made it to her home. Marian led the conversation.

"We sat him down and said that there had been a big accident and that Daddy had gone to the accident, and that it was very serious and that he was lost, but there were a lot of people looking for him—a lot of really important people with big trucks and cranes," Jason said. "He whispered in her ear at one point after she kind of explained it and said, 'Can we go look for him?' And she said, no, that there were people that were looking for him that could do it better. And then he went and got a stuffed animal from his bed for each of us to make us feel better. He could see that we were all sad."

After about a week, Jason returned to his job at a Midtown restaurant, and he slept in his own bed more nights than he spent at Marian's. But the rest of his hours remained devoted to Marian's and Aidan's care. Her sister, another friend, and Jason cleaned Marian's refrigerator and her closets. They arranged for play dates and transportation for Aidan.

Right now, said Jason, "You can't ask anything of Marian. And so that is something we're able to do—just be there 100 percent for her." The other two generally stay through the night. "And I go home, and then I wake up and come back."

"I know one of my traits is that I am a good friend. And I felt like this was really my chance to let that take flight. Every day I wake up and have to restructure my priorities because I still forget every morning that everything is different and that I'm not my first priority anymore. And that's fine. That's how it needs to be," Jason said.

But it is a role that drastically altered Jason's daily rituals.

"I'm a single, thirty-three-year-old gay male," he said. "I had a pretty typical gay urban life that was pretty self-centered—a lot of primping, a lot of me, a lot of dates and talking about boys and superficial fun time and working out, going to therapy. . . . A lot of that has fallen away. And it seems completely superficial at this point.

"It's amazing that I've been able to be as selfless as I have. I'm very generous in general, but not in this way. This is a whole other level. Every day is another challenge for me to say, 'You know what? I can't go tan today; I can't work out today. It's fine. It doesn't matter. This is more important.' And it is.

"I wish it were easier; that's what I wish. I think of all those saints who say, 'Oh, I so selflessly gave myself up to take care of the sick or the needy or my friend' or this and that. I mean, I do it, and I do it gratefully, but I tell you, it's hard. Every day is a challenge to show up and be present. Once I'm there, it's fine. I have so much love for her and so much compassion and so much wonder and gratitude, in a way, to behold this experience—to see her get through it and do it with such grace, because she has been phenomenal, and it's almost a miracle to see someone survive this."

Jason had planned to have a family, and his new role in Marian's life left him wondering whether this would be the one. Even in the early days, when his mom asked him what she could do from California, he told her, in half jest, that she might have a grandchild to help raise.

"I feel like I'm preparing for a major adjustment. I live close by. I feel like it's going to be up to me, her sister, and a couple of other friends in the neighborhood to really be her support for the long haul, and I've told her that, and I'm totally there for the long haul. In my mind, I'm picturing being very involved. I don't know if she'll need it when it gets further down the line," Jason said. "I do have room in my life for it, so I feel like maybe this is destiny or something."

A Worchester, England, firefighter led a fundraising campaign across two counties that has netted approximately $70,000 for victims' families. "As a firefighter, when the bells toll I know what it feels like," he said.

Marty Glembotzky, WABC-TV

TWELVE HOURS, A HALF-DAY, A LIFETIME...

Kathleen Avino

When I woke up on September 11, 2001, the pain in my hip felt like a knife had found a home. But my thinking is simple; if I can make it to the shower I can make it to work. With lupus and several bad discs in my spine, this isn't always as easy as it may sound. I showered and dressed. I grabbed a couple of lunch drinks and several pieces of fruit. I had bought the fruit the night before for my project superintendent, Nick. Nick feeds me all the time and never lets me pay, so to return his many kindnesses I buy fruit whenever I remember. I never imagined as I filled the bag with apples, grapes, and plums, how precious that fruit would become.

I started the car, since subways are out of the question for me for health reasons. I only made it one block before I encountered my first obstacle. A double-parked car blocked the side street. I beeped my horn and pointed that I could not pass. Her kind and considerate response was that she didn't give a ★★★★. Angry in return, I questioned what kind of people we had become.

I raced against time. My other adage is if you manage to get out of bed on time don't be stupid enough to be late. I didn't get very far. The traffic was a mess and at a standstill. As the traffic reporter droned about the back roads of New Jersey traffic, I crept along. With my choices being memorizing the license plate in front of me or looking at the Manhattan skyline, I naturally choose my beautiful city and its vertical works of art. I was born here, have lived here most of my life, and I never tire of its majesty.

I arrived at the construction trailer where I work a mere five minutes late. Our trailer is located on North End Avenue and Murray Street, approximately two and a half blocks from the World Trade Center. We were all stressed out over finishing the steel rebar placement in the concrete slab for our project. We were a week late with the concrete pour, which was scheduled for the next day. We were determined to make the opening of the Irish Hunger Memorial for St. Patrick's Day in March. In retrospect, it was lucky the pour was delayed. The streets would have been clogged with a long line of concrete trucks.

I walked into Nick's office. It's in the front of the trailer and has a window with a clear shot of the Twin Towers. As I looked out the window I watched the upper façade of the tower fold inward and saw a silver fin enter the hole. Next came the boom, and a shuddering of the trailer, the fireball, and then the black smoke engulfing the entire upper floors of the building.

I did not feel or hear my scream; it was as if someone else had lost their mind, not me. I was frozen in place staring out the window, with that strange sound coming out of me. I frantically dialed 911, with no luck. I dialed the operator and got a recording. I dialed my husband at Fire Department headquarters and when I heard him answer that screaming began again.

I calmed down enough to call my stepdaughter in Texas to say I was okay. I was so glad I called, hearing such relief in her voice. Meanwhile, the street was filled with confused and terrified souls. Many begged to use our phone to reassure their loved ones. It was an easy enough kindness. A young police officer, visibly shaken, asked to use the phone. We nodded; he dialed, listened then hung up. He stared out and said to no one in particular, "My wife is up there. I think I just lost my wife," and went outside teary and stunned. I returned to my office and phoned my daughter's school and then my mother. As I spoke to my mother on the phone, she screamed that there was another plane. Fear ripped through me because I couldn't see another plane. Panic raced through me as to where it was and how close. I didn't wonder for too long. I watched once again a huge gold and black fireball blow from the side of the second tower. I felt as though death had wrapped its arms around me and laughed in my face.

The number of stunned people in the street increased in waves. Nick and I quickly went to the job site to make sure all the men were all right. We instructed them to grab their gear and head home. Once we were sure no one was left, we locked up all the equipment as best we could, locked the gates, and headed back to the trailer. People were everywhere, slowly heading north. There was, surprisingly, no panic. Not yet anyway.

We snaked our way back to the trailer and retreated inside. We heard a popping sound, then without further warning, a once monumental symbol of power and strength, the first of the twin towers slid, as though on rails, straight down to the ground. Its final good-bye was a gray billowy cloud rising up to the top covering the roof. I found myself crouched on the floor sobbing, knowing at that split second it wasn't over.

Why was I feeling so devastated? I had grown up with television. I have "seen" disasters occur all over the globe and on American soil. Why then? I had been insulated in the past, because I had seen it with the protection of the glass and the metal housing. Here there was no safety buffer. I couldn't change the channel and watch something else. I was forced to watch, to feel. Forced to watch the fires, feel the vibration, feel the fear, feel the heat, and as the dust approached, smell the death.

Nick was outside again. Suddenly the remaining tower seemed to tilt. Once again, a strange sound blew past my ears. This time I was screaming for Nick to get back in the trailer. Dear God, it's coming for us. I watched as if in slow motion, it fell over. This is such a simple statement, if you're talking about a lamp or a bicycle. A 110-story building just fell over and a 20-story gray and black cloud of fury was heading straight for us.

Within a second, the trailer filled with emergency personnel from every federal, state, and city agency, huddling as a single unit, holding, touching, silently praying God would spare us. Then suddenly everything went from being bathed in bright sunshine to pitch black darkness. And then the pinging sound started as dust, papers, and other debris smashed into the walls of the trailer. That's when I learned minutes could last an eternity. My daughter's face flashed in front of me. I pleaded with God, "Not again." Her birth mother had been taken from her in Russia many years ago; I could not let that happen again. She was the reason I had to survive.

Slowly flashlight beams darted around, voices became urgent and the light began to filter in. I opened my eyes to a surreal scene of stunned, blank faces, as I was once again lifted off the floor. Gray uniforms once blue. I was in a sea of walking ghosts with gray-caked faces and hollow eyes. We began a wet paper towel brigade from the water cooler to wash faces and burning eyes. I darted from face to face. I was grateful to do something to get my mind off my beautiful city disappearing before my eyes. Expressionless faces managing twisted smiles as I handed out plums, grapes, and apples. They mumbled thanks and gave automated nods. It wasn't much, but it seemed to help. I was glad to be snapped back to something familiar and normal. Sharing some food with some nice people.

One firefighter became my salvation. He was badly covered in the ashes, especially his eyes. He could not see. Construction first-aid kits always include eyewash as standard items. I thanked God for that sight-saving bottle ready to be of service in that little metal box. I washed his eyes and tried to keep him calm. His buddy kept checking on him and reassuring him he needed to stay put.

Meanwhile, we doled out water from my coffee mug because we had run out of paper cups the day before. I could not miss the symbolism of that one coffee cup being passed from person to person, providing life-giving liquid. Rescue personnel floated in and out of our trailer for the next few hours using the phones and toilets, and washing the dust from their eyes. I watched seasoned, trained professionals with tears more from emotion than from irritation.

By this time Nick, Mark, the equipment operator, and I were about the last civilians in the area of Ground Zero. I couldn't leave because the pinched nerve in my back prevented me from walking any long distance. Nick, God bless him, wouldn't leave me, and Mark knew he'd be needed to operate the debris moving equipment. So we decided to wait for the bridges to be reopened, figuring we'd drive out when given the chance. We were also hungry, so we ventured out into the desolation. Everything was covered in ash.

I remember remarking to Nick that the ash was a very scary omen. My nickname, Kat, comes from the saying that a cat has nine lives. I have almost died six times, including three allergic reactions, which put me into anaphylactic shock. One attack was as recent as two weeks ago. I remembered vividly the feeling of my eyes, ears, and finally my throat closing. The desperate cry you can't utter for help because your voice has been sealed in swollen tissue. All you can do is sit in terror and pray that someone comes soon. Is that what was happening to hundreds and maybe thousands of people right now? I looked down once again at the fine powder attaching itself to my shoes and legs. I feared the next time I saw such a gray ash I would get cheated out of my remaining three lives.

The trees were filled with pieces of partially charred letters, memos, tax returns, and receipts. We picked up some of the papers and read some of the names, wondering if they had made it or not. The silence was eerie.

We brought food and drinks and walked back to our box of safety. We ate and we watched the end of something. Exactly what, at the time, I wasn't sure. I am still not sure. Had we lost our innocence maybe, our complete sense of security maybe, our invincibility, absolutely. When something ends one prays it will be replaced by something better. Let's pray that our losses weren't in vain.

A deadly stillness hung over us and drifted by us. Even the smoke rising above the pulverized pile of buildings, machinery, and people seemed to lift in slow motion. I started to feel nothing at all. I started to feel this non-reality sucking me into a non-place. I felt alone, lost, and very numb. This scared me more than all that had just happened. I wanted to go home, like I never wanted to go home before.

On our next trip out, we spotted two suitcases just standing by themselves. Once begrudgingly pulled by their owners, they were now little orphans waiting to be rescued. I decided, Why not do a good deed? Nick was rightfully nervous that it might be filled with explosives. But I had seen the police dogs make several passes. They did not seem concerned, so I convinced Nicky that we should each grab one and put it in the trailer for safekeeping. Silently hoping I would have someone to return them to. Inside the little pocket on the outside of one of the bags was a business card for a woman from Boston. I called her office and was happy to hear that she had gotten out via ferry to New Jersey. She was four months pregnant and attending a conference, but made it out in one piece. I smiled, pleased with myself that I had made someone happy who had been so recently filled with fear. She had her life, her baby's life, and now she had her clothes.

At 5:00 P.M. we decided we had had enough. We had no electricity and the thought of staying overnight was frightening. We knew the bridges had been reopened. I brushed off enough ashes from the car windshield to see and proceeded to take on New York's finest. The worst that would happen would be to be forced back from whence I came. I was determined to go home; I had earned that right. I made it as far as Broadway and made a wrong turn into a group of tired, stressed-out police officers who were not happy to see me. But after rolling down the window, they got a better look at my condition and anger swiftly changed to compassion. They got me to the Brooklyn Bridge and I left the gates of hell behind me. Driving over the bridge, I thanked God again for sparing me, and prayed for the children who would ask in a few hours "Where's Mommy?" or "Where's Daddy?"

When I finally arrived home, my tree in the front yard looked greener and my house strong and welcoming. As I climbed the steps to my front door, I suddenly realized the pain from the pinched nerve had miraculously vanished. I could walk without pain. All I could wonder was how things would have been so different if the pain had not been there this morning. We would have left and the trailer would not have offered so much refuge to so many. I regret placing Nick in harm's way, but we did make a difference. At least I hope so.

I washed the remaining dust from my burning skin and awaited the arrival of my daughter. She had been picked up from school, fed and cared for by a dear friend. A Moslem woman who has become part of our family. She sent not only my daughter home but also two large containers of food ready to be eaten. Seeing my daughter's face for that first moment did more to wash away the horror than all the showers I may take for the rest of my life or all the time I would take to try and forget.

The phone never stopped ringing for the next two days. I never realized I was so loved. I never realized, I, a nobody, mattered to so many people. I never realized before how many paths of others we cross and somehow enrich in our day-to-day lives. I never realized our immense responsibility for how we conduct ourselves and how much we can influence others. I never realized how little we understand the depth of our need for each other. I do now.

I called a few Moslem friends and offered reassurance that my feelings toward them had not changed and was given comfort and prayers in return. Some may consider me a fool. Are we foolish not to hate? Are we not all Americans and do we not all bleed red? We must not forget this. Although American lives were taken, we must not, we cannot let them take the American spirit.

Every religion on the face of the Earth has the equivalent of the Lord's

Prayer. Their books of worship contain passages that encourage their followers to forgive. Every Sunday millions on bended knee recite in unison "Forgive us our trespasses as we forgive those who trespass against us." At this time even I cannot forgive the monsters that perpetrated such evil unto the world. I want justice, not revenge. It is this difference that makes America, America. But I do hope we do not twist our deep-seated grief and anger into poisonous hatred. Because hatred is a double-edged sword. As you use hatred to destroy your enemy you also destroy yourself, and you cannot be "delivered from evil." You instead make yourself part of the evil. Each person in the world must make their own choice, with the understanding that with their choice they have the power to make a difference. We all make a difference.

Now we slowly claw our way back to normalcy. Probably never making it back to where we started. Let's just pray that wherever we end up, we will be in a better, healthier, and more peaceful place than the place we left behind. Let's pray that we will be better, healthier, and more at peace.

> Emily, a four-year-old from Houston, bugged her parents during the week of the 11th to go to the Red Cross. Busy with other things, her parents kept delaying the visit. They relented when Emily said, "My heart hurts."

The Prudential Spirit of Community Awards

I CARE ABOUT YOU

Annie Wignall has been giving since well before September 2001. Indeed, this thirteen-year-old from Newton, Iowa, has been caring for children in need since January 2000. "I started when I was eleven. My mom came home from a meeting from her job and told me that they needed people to collect shampoo and things like that for foster- and crisis-care kids," Annie said. "I thought it would be neat if we could do something bigger and better than that." That's the day Care Bags was born, a nonprofit organization that creates bags of essentials for children in need.

Annie's organization has mobilized legions of donors, both businesses and individuals, to provide the raw materials for her work. Volunteers nationwide sew bags, bibs, and blankets to mail to Iowa, where the bags are filled with toothpaste, soap, and "things that I know that they would like." For babies, there are bottles and receiving blankets. For young children, books or stuffed animals might be tucked inside. And teens often find journals awaiting their thoughts.

When Annie, an eighth-grader, learned about the terrorist attacks, "I saw there were kids on TV, and I wanted to do something to help them," she said. "And so I thought it would be good to send my Care Bags to them."

Even before September 11, the Care Bags organization had drawn help from volunteer distributors. Twenty-two agencies move the bags to eighty towns in Iowa and to other states for disaster relief. And Airline Ambassadors—a nonprofit group whose members hand-deliver humanitarian aid—distributes Annie's bags throughout the world.

So Care Bags arranged to have the Salvation Army and the Airline Ambassadors deliver bags to New York and Washington, D.C., for any children affected by the attacks. Production has increased from about sixty bags to about ninety a month in response.

The Wignalls later found out that Jim Cleere, a family friend, was among the missing at the World Trade Center.

Annie's mother, Cathy Wignall, said Annie is realistic about how much solace her bags can provide against terrorist attacks. But Cathy sees Annie's commitment as a critical part of citizenship. "I think we all have a part to play in the world and in making the world a better place," Cathy said. "If Annie's work encourages other kids to do something like it or to start something of their own, that's cool. Maybe they'll make one little kid feel better. That's what really matters."

Each bag that Care Bags makes carries a poem by Annie on the outside:

This little bag was made especially for you
To say I think you're special and I care about you, too.
Inside you'll find a bunch of things like toothpaste, soap or toy.
I collected all this stuff for you to fill your heart with joy.
I hope this makes you happy today and everyday,
And remember someone loves you in a very special way.

Your friend, Annie Wignall

Care Bags Foundation
c/o Annie Wignall
623 East 17th Street N.
Newton, Iowa 50208
Phone: 641-792-5037 (please ask for Cathy)
E-mail: mw@pcpartner.net
Web site: www.carebags.org

Residents of the Grace House Union Mission, a homeless shelter in Savannah, Georgia, collected $52 for victims' families.

CHAPTER 14

Melissa DeMerit

BUTTERFLY MESSAGE

Susan C. DeMerit

The morning was just beginning for me when we received a phone call from my husband's brother telling us to turn on the television. Little did I know this would be "The Day the World Stood Still."

All day I had the small television on in my office. Employees would stop and watch in horror and helplessness. None of us could bear to see what was happening to our country and all the innocent people for more than a few minutes, leaving with inevitable tears of sorrow.

The world was disturbingly quiet. No planes, no helicopters, so few phone calls, little traffic. The birds that usually visit me were nowhere in sight.

There were, however, glimmers that kept reappearing at my second-story window—white butterflies. Not just one, but many throughout the day, like little white angels drifting past my window.

As people appeared in my office, they would watch the television for a moment, and then I would point out the white butterflies. They would smile and leave. The smiles were small, but the impact was great. They were the calming, soothing reality that we must not give up. They were the small reminders of just how important it is to give freely, just like the white angelic butterflies.

At the Salvation Army center in lower Manhattan, twenty-five volunteers from AT&T's Basking Ridge offices busied themselves making 5,000 sandwiches to restock the Manhattan canteens. Nearby sat bread racks loaded with sandwiches in wax paper, sealed with Post-It notes from children—tributes and messages of encouragement to firefighters.

CHAPTER 15

Nicholos Wethington, Omar Tesdell, Laura Hatfield

Brenda Welchlin

A TIME FOR PEACE

*O*mar Tesdell is a pacifist who comes from a family of pacifists. He also comes from a line of Palestinians who were forced out of their home when Israel was created. His paternal grandparents were Quakers from Iowa with a passion for the Middle East. Shortly after they were married, they went to work in a refugee camp in the Gaza Strip with a group from the American Friends Service Committee working with the United Nations.

"That was a pretty big influence in my life, that coming through my dad, and then also hearing about my mom's story growing up," Omar said. "Arab residents of my mother's town, Lydd, were forced from their homes between July 10 and 12, 1948," when the state of Israel was being created. "My mom's family was forced out of their house and fled their home in Palestine to another part of the West Bank and then to a town in Jordan and then finally to Amman, Jordan, which is where my mother grew up."

Omar's parents met in Jordan, where his dad was working for a newspaper and teaching English classes. They married and moved to Iowa, where Omar's dad returned to school. Omar was born in Ames, but soon moved with his family to Saudi Arabia for five years, until his family moved once again to Iowa.

Omar had been to Jordan as a child to visit his mother's siblings. He and his brother, both holding U.S. passports, were once passed through a border checkpoint and then left alone when their mother's entrance was delayed because of the Palestinian city listed as her birthplace. As a teen, he visited relatives in the West Bank, where several male cousins of his told stories of being stopped, harassed, and sometimes jailed because of their heritage.

In the summer of 2001, just before his sophomore year of college, Omar lived for more than two months with his aunts in Jordan, writing for a newspaper and improving his Arabic. And after getting permission from his father, he paid a visit to another aunt who was still in the West Bank. Although the neighborhood was perfectly calm during his short stay, it was evident that it was often a war zone.

"I've seen the effects of violence, and I can't see any good coming from reacting to violence with more violence," he said. But he had done little with his convictions beyond sharing with friends over dinner his seemingly far-fetched vision of a peaceful Israeli–Palestinian resolution.

The morning of September 11, after learning of the day's attacks, Omar ran into his friend, Nicholos Wethington, on the campus of Iowa State University. Nick, a sophomore from Rapid City, South Dakota, and Omar shared many political views. They made plans to get together that evening just to talk about the day's events. After a vigil on campus, they rounded up ten people to meet in a residence hall lounge at 10:30 P.M.

The conversation quickly turned to action, and by the time the group disbanded, it had a name—Time for Peace—and four key belief statements focusing on nonviolent resolution, investigation, and rebuilding. By the next day, it had a logo, printed flyers, a Web site, and an e-mail list.

"The swiftness with which we were able to mobilize was incredible," said Laura Hatfield, a junior at Iowa State whose parents had protested environmental issues as students in the late 1970s and early '80s. "Pretty much my whole life disappeared for about two weeks."

"We're still recovering academically," Omar said.

For all three, the events of September 11 provided the transition from thought to action. "I have been of a very liberal mindset my whole life," Laura said. "I just never had the opportunity to put that into action. The lament of our generation up until September 11 was that we had no common cause behind which to really rally and unite as young people."

And it was Omar's first active stance, too, spurred along in part by his mother's death from cancer the previous December. "It's part of the reason why I was driven by this, just because I felt like I was pretty powerless in her death."

Time for Peace began organizing weekly vigils and taking steps to educate people on campus. "Part of our role is just to provide an alternative to people who receive only messages from the mainstream media and the government, which are all saying we're at war," Laura said. "And if you're undecided about it and that's the only message you receive, that's what you're going to go with."

The group held a meeting at the city library to expand to the off-campus community, and the students found a wealth of wisdom shared by adults who had protested during the Vietnam and Persian Gulf wars. Time for Peace held postcard drives and role-playing sessions to consider how to respond to challenges from other people without letting those interactions escalate.

They used that open-minded approach with a senator they thought would be an adversary. A state representative who had expressed interest in the group suggested that some members attend a unity rally that Sen. Tom Harkin was attending.

"We had intended to go to protest, but after hearing Harkin speak, we realized that his viewpoint was very much in line with what we were saying," Laura said. "He wasn't taking a nonviolent stance, but it was definitely a really moderate stance. And so afterward we said let's not protest his rally but rather join and stand on the same side of the street with them and greet people as they're coming in and be part of the unity—but express it in a way that there can be unity not for war but just unity for doing the right thing, remembering the victims."

Omar and the rest of the group hope to extend that sense of unity, even if it means dissolution of their organization. "We've kind of called ourselves a group, an organization, but really—I think this was echoed by other people—wanted to be part of a movement that's larger than any groups starting up on individual campuses," Omar said. "We don't even care if we keep our name or anything, if we become part of a larger group. It's not about our group. It's about nonviolence."

> Escaping the fire at the World Trade Center, Michael Benfante and a coworker carried a woman in a wheelchair down 68 flights of stairs to safety.

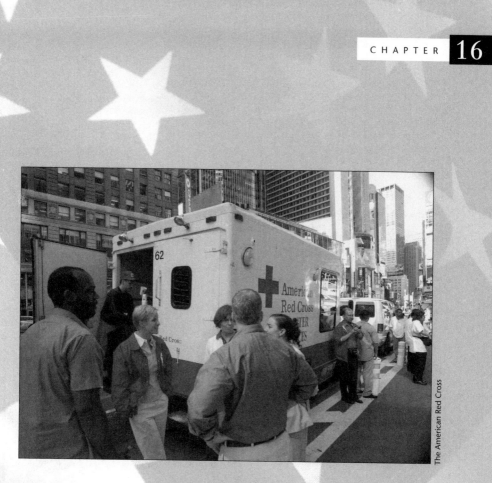

CHAPTER 16

The American Red Cross

BEGINNING ANEW

John Larkin, Staff Writer, *redcross.org*

*C*ole Bell, twenty-five, had been living in New York City for three weeks, having recently moved from his hometown of Miami, Florida. On the morning of September 11, he and a friend enjoyed an early breakfast near the World Trade Center. After they chatted for awhile, Cole walked his friend to the elevator, said good-bye, and headed for his job at Rockefeller Center. Minutes later, the planes struck the buildings, and Cole has not seen his friend since.

Cole was walking through the mall area below the Twin Towers on his way to work when tragedy struck. His life was spared, but he was severely disoriented by the trauma of the event. "At first, I was dazed," said Cole. "I wandered around for days." Tuesday and Wednesday night, he slept in a church, spending his days walking around the city, not saying much of anything to anyone. He spent the next night sleeping in Union Square, where hundreds of people have been maintaining a constant vigil since the tragedy occurred. While in Union Square, he noticed a sign, posted by a local acupuncturist, offering his services for free. "I said to myself, 'Boy do I need this.'"

After hearing Cole's story, the practitioner suggested that he go to an American Red Cross shelter around the corner. Cole followed the acupuncturist's advice and set up temporary residence at the Washington Irving shelter. There, he found a place where he could sort things out and allow some structure to return to his life.

"Everybody was really nice, especially Sue, a [Red Cross volunteer] mental health counselor from Roosevelt Hospital," Cole said. Sue spends evenings at Washington Irving, listening while residents talk about their experiences and work through their emotions regarding the disaster.

Cole plans to volunteer for the Red Cross "when things get back to normal. . . . I'd like to volunteer for disaster relief work—perhaps organize something company-wide, through my work," he said. Cole is no stranger to volunteering. He organized blood drives in high school and served as a local disaster volunteer during Hurricane Andrew. Cole is sold on both the Red Cross and on remaining in New York City, despite frequent, subtle requests from his family to return to Miami.

After three nights in the shelter, Cole was eager to return to his job at the sales department of J. Crew. He admits, though, that he has to keep himself busy in order to stay focused. "When I first got here, I started making all the beds," he said smiling. After having a chance to rest and collect his thoughts, he is ready to begin anew, which is exactly what he will need to do. His apartment is located on the 100 block of Gateway Plaza. "It had a great view of the World Trade Center," he said.

Nurse Patty Higgins never imagined that collecting blood would include flying to the nation's capital in a private jet, escorted by FBI F-16 fighter planes. She was one of four Kansans asked to assist in the massive blood collection effort in the Washington, D.C., area due to the outpouring of generosity from volunteer blood donors following the terrorist attacks. Raytheon Aircraft Company, which lost four employees in the Pentagon and World Trade Center plane crashes, donated a private jet so that Higgins and her colleagues could get to Washington and draw blood from the thousands of eager volunteers.

CHAPTER 17

Freddie Lieberman

HELPING ANY WAY
WE CAN

*C*indy Bahnij knew the crew of American Airlines flight 77. She had flown that route as a domestic flight attendant based in Washington, D.C., before switching to international flights out of New York's John F. Kennedy International Airport.

But she was home ironing the morning of September 11, with the television on in the background. A special news report cut in, and she watched the second plane hit the second tower of the World Trade Center.

"At that moment, I knew in my heart it was a terrorist attack," Cindy said. When her daughter called to tell her the Pentagon had been hit, it only solidified her belief.

In the days to come, she learned which of her friends had been on the flight that crashed into the Pentagon. There were Ken and Jennifer Lewis, a flight attendant couple who were so often together that they were known as "Kennifer."

There was David Charlebois, a top gun fighter pilot in the Navy. He was already a hero—a Reservist as well. At his memorial service, a friend shared a story of when Dave had given up on a friend who was running late for a lunch appointment. He bought a sandwich to go, then met his friend as he walked out of the restaurant. Dave quickly handed his untouched sandwich to a homeless man and returned inside to order lunch with his friend.

Cindy talked with her daughter about how they could possibly respond to such loss, and the two considered donating blood. Overnight Tuesday, Cindy knew it needed to be more than a family effort. "Why don't we see if we can get American Airlines flight attendants, cockpit crew, whoever could come help to give blood—and come in uniform," Cindy said. "If we came in uniform and marched in, all of America would know—and the bad people would know—that we're here, we're fighting, we're arm in arm, and we're going to help in any way we can."

Wednesday morning, Cindy called some friends who were flight attendants, and she called local television stations. When they didn't broadcast her call to action, she called back until they did. By 6 P.M., more than sixty flight attendants and crew members were in line to donate blood—and they were in uniform.

"I was very proud how fast we could muster that big a group in such a short time. When we walked in, dressed in our uniforms, the civilians there stood up and applauded. We were moved by their support of us. It was the very least we could do," Cindy said.

Besides the American Airlines employees, workers from United Airlines and U.S. Airways had heeded the call and lined up in solidarity. "What we did was so little. But it was a way to put one foot in front of the other and keep going. It's a way we can remember the thousands we've lost. And it was our way of letting the world know we're moving forward, and we're only going to be better than we ever were," Cindy said. "The comfort in this tragedy is how we have all come together, dug our heels in, and reached out to help."

Cindy drew strength, too, from the family of David Charlebois, one of her friends on the plane. "Sherry, his wife, is the epitome of courage and bravery. She attended many of the other crew's memorials with head-to-toe pristine professionalism and bravery and courage. She's a model for all of us. When I saw her walk into another flight attendant's memorial, respecting everyone else and not thinking of her own grief, I thought to myself, 'How can we not help when we see that kind of giving?'"

Bethany Jones and her British husband Leighton joined the Salvation Army relief effort in New York, fresh from a Lake Tahoe honeymoon. Leighton's parents in Bristol, England, have relayed to him the mood back home. "Their impression is, this didn't just happen to New York; it happened to everybody."

Bright Horizons

STUDENTS PITCH IN

Becky Orfinger, Staff Writer, *redcross.org*

*I*t takes at least five hours to drive from Ithaca, New York, to New York City. But the distance didn't stop Danfung Dennis, Tim Wells, and Tyler Kaune, three Cornell University students, from jumping into a car and heading to the Big Apple as soon as they heard about the terrorist attacks on the World Trade Center. Their mission: To donate blood as close to the site of the tragedy as they could, so that their blood would likely go to victims of the disaster.

"We left Ithaca just a few hours after the attacks, when we first heard the request for blood. I couldn't just sit and watch the horror on television—I had to do something to help," said Danfung. "Class and track practice didn't really matter. We just grabbed the map and some cookies and hopped in the car." Once the threesome got to New Jersey, they stopped at every hospital they saw, hoping to donate blood. But they visited six hospitals and were turned away from each one because so many people were in line to donate. Once it got dark, they decided to spend the night in a Jersey City park across the street from one of the hospitals that they visited.

In the morning, the three took some pictures of the smoky Manhattan skyline (Jersey City is across the Hudson River from New York City) and headed back up to Ithaca. But on the way, they found the American Red Cross Northeastern Pennsylvania Blood Services Region in Wilkes-Barre. The Red Cross staff there was thrilled with the group's long-distance trip and immediately ushered them into the donor room. Molly Groody, a spokesperson for the Northeastern Pennsylvania blood region, said her colleagues were "touched that these young men would go to such great lengths to give blood."

But these three Cornell students are only one example of altruistic behavior being exhibited nationwide. On campuses all over the country, college students are putting schoolwork, social engagements, and sports aside to help their peers—and the rest of America—recover from the terrorist attacks.

Virtually every university in the United States marked the events of September 11 in some way—by canceling classes, holding a vigil, planning emergency blood drives, or providing grief counseling. Multi-religion daily prayer gatherings were offered at Duke University in Durham, North Carolina, for grieving students and community members, and discussion forums to address students reactions to terrorism and the current situation in the country were planned.

At Princeton, the tragedy was personal, as eight victims of the attacks have been identified as Princeton University graduates. Hoping to reach as many current and past Princetonians as possible, the university organized a response center, said Jessie Washington, special projects manager in the Office of the Vice President for Campus Life and a former Red Cross volunteer. "In the days following the attacks, we had a physical location for the response center in the University Campus Center, a hotline phone number, a Web site and a special e-mail address for concerned students, alumni, and members of the community," said Washington. "We also worked with other campus groups to provide religious services, counseling opportunities and information about scheduling concerns. Many friends and alumni called to check on former classmates who worked in the New York area."

Sally El-Sadek, president of the Princeton University Arab Society, organized a "teach-in" to provide students, staff and faculty with a political and historical perspective on the attacks. Professors from various academic departments were invited to teach and lead discussion sections during the event. Several undergraduates also organized a peace rally on campus.

In addition, the Princeton community referred qualified mental health counselors to help with recovery efforts in New York and Washington. All Red Cross volunteers in the wake of this disaster were given free tickets to Princeton football games to thank them for their tireless efforts. "The Red Cross also taught me how to use and support relief operation volunteers," said Washington. "People want to help, but they must be trained, fed, and acknowledged along the way."

In support, a construction worker in Paterson, New Jersey, painted the outside of his home into an American flag.

Major Donnie K. Smith   Al Marchand

GOOD-BYE, DEAR FRIEND

*D*onnie Smith, a Hobbs, New Mexico, policeman for the past twenty-one years, first met Al Marchand when both men reported for training at the New Mexico Law Enforcement Academy in 1980. Upon learning that Marchand, a retired policeman, was killed while working as a flight attendant on a flight that crashed into the World Trade Center, Smith wrote the following letter to his friend, then read it at a community memorial service:

Dear Al,

I vividly remember the day twenty-one years ago when we met. I was facing the next six weeks away from my new bride, homesick, nervous, and depressed. You walked up in your confident way and said, "Al Marchand," and offered a hand. Without knowing it, I had just met a friend whom I would respect and admire for the rest of my life.

Six weeks for us to become competent, capable police officers. But we pulled together and made it. We were all young, cocky, and so terribly naïve. We had no way of knowing what kind of evil was out there. But we would learn.

The passing weeks soon turned to years. Countless nights on the street, arresting criminals, fighting drunks, and facing down menacing bullies while our families were at home alone. Working on Thanksgiving and Christmas while others enjoyed the holidays with their loved ones; missing our kids' ball games and school programs—but, hey, that's life for a cop.

Many of those we knew from the early days seemed to drift away. Many left the profession for better jobs. But there were a few like us who stuck it out. Over the years we saw each from time to time, usually at some type of training and at many police officer funerals. All too often, we were just too busy to notice the time that was passing.

I'm told now that you too have left us. I don't know that I'll ever understand why things happen as they do—you, a devoted family man, a respected and loved member of your community, a person who made all the sacrifices. You had done your time and should be enjoying the part of life that you worked so hard to get to.

I watched the pictures of what I now know was your airplane crashing into that magnificent building. It's ironic that I've stood atop that very tower in awe at the marvels man is capable of.

I think now, I see a different side of humanity. Since yours was the second plane to strike, maybe you had some idea of what was to come. But I will never know. When I think about you in that situation, I am reminded of a line from the Police Officers Survival Creed that says, "Never, never, never give up."

I know you held true to that creed. I know you fought the good fight. I know that at whatever point your life slipped away, you were still raging against the fading of the light.

I don't mind telling you, Al, I'm angry. And sad. This should not have happened in our country, and it should not have happened to you.

It should not have happened to any of the thousands of good and decent people that died with you. There were many brave brothers and sisters who lost their lives that day while just doing their job. At least there is some comfort in knowing that you died among those who stood for the same things you did.

I am so privileged to have known you and been able to share precious time with you. As the weeks turn to months and then to years, the American people will not soon forget.

And I promise, Al, I will never forget. Rest in peace, my friend.

A fund has been set up to assist Al Marchand's three children. Mail contributions to:

Children of Al Marchand Education Trust
The First National Bank
414 Tenth Street
Alamogordo NM 88310

While rescue workers searched through the rubble, they had two unlikely companions—Tikva, a two-year-old Keeshound, and Kate, a three-year-old yellow Labrador retriever. The pooches are part of the Hope Crisis and Response Team working with the American Red Cross, which brought emotional support to those affected by the attacks. Supported by the Delta Society, a nonprofit organization "dedicated to improving human health through service and therapy animals," Tikva and Kate are two of four dogs working in New York City with their handlers.

CHAPTER 20

The Everett *Daily Herald* by Stephanie S. Cordle

TEENS WITH HELPING HANDS

Mary Harvey, Scholastic

On the morning of September 11, 2001, Jack Kirkland was worried about gym class. "It was the first day of gym, and I'd forgotten my gym shorts," the thirteen-year-old New York City student said. His friend Niki Achitoff-Gray was wondering if she'd make the swim team. Julia Baskin, another friend, was thinking about a class history project.

In one split-second, life was dramatically and forever changed for these freshmen at Stuyvesant High School, just blocks from where the city's beloved "Twin Towers" had stood. Their city was swept with despair and grief in the wake of the world's worst terrorist attack. And they wanted to do something about it.

As shaken as they were after having fled the scene of destruction that Tuesday morning, by Thursday, this group of teens had a plan: Hold a bake sale and donate the money to a fund that supports the firefighters and rescue workers hard at work.

Jack, Julia, Niki, and their friend Abena Mackall baked cookies, brownies, and cupcakes. They made posters and flyers, stating who they were and what they were doing. They even came up with a name for themselves: TINY, or Teens Improving New York.

"Everyone says they feel so helpless and they don't know what to do," said Julia, fourteen. "In school, we've always had bake sales to raise money, so we thought, 'Why not?'"

They set up their goods on a folding table near a Tower Records store on a busy New York street and began asking for donations. "Please help firemen and rescue workers who are working around the clock," they said to curious passersby. "This is the way you can make a difference, this is the way we can make a difference."

"When a lot of our friends saw what we were doing, they said, 'Oh, that's a great idea, we'll call people and we'll get other people involved too,'" Julia said. "They wanted it to grow, they wanted to help too." In the coming days, several friends from other schools showed up to help and lend support.

In just the first two days, TINY raised more than $600 for the New York Times 9/11 Neediest Fund, which aids firefighters, rescue workers, victims, and their families.

"I saw out the window in class what was going on. It made the four of us really want to do something to help," said Niki, fourteen, who had gone with her friends first to the Red Cross to offer help, but had been asked to come back later due to an outpouring of volunteers. "I think it's bringing out a lot of the good in New York City because everybody is really joining together and pulling their own weight and trying to help everyone in their own lives."

"I was out here all day yesterday and I almost lost my voice," said Abena, fourteen, on the second day of the sale. "But I've just got to keep on doing it, because it's all that I can do."

More than 1,000 folks attended a candlelight vigil in Grayslake, Illinois, which has a population of only 18,506.

CHAPTER 21

Prayer at NYC memorial, *Los Angeles Times* Photo by Gary Friedman

HIS PARISH KNEW NO BOUNDS

Ricardo Alonso-Zaldivar, *Los Angeles Times*

Rev. Mychal Judge, the New York City Fire Department chaplain who died ministering at the scene of the September 11 terrorist attacks and whose funeral was the following Saturday, was well known for his compassionate care for families of air crash victims.

In 1996 the Franciscan priest became the personal pastor to many families of victims of the TWA Flight 800 disaster off Long Island, regardless of their religious affiliation. Judge spent weeks at a Ramada hotel that became the base of operations for the families, and he remained involved in some of their lives until his death at the World Trade Center.

Judge was killed while administering last rites to a badly injured firefighter. After taking off his helmet to pray, he was hit by falling debris. A *Los Angeles Times* reporter researching an article on support services for families of air crash victims interviewed Judge in 2000, and he spoke of his efforts to be a healing presence for people whose lives had been torn apart.

"In seminary, you can get all the theology and Scripture in the world, and you land in your first parish, and you find out it's you—the personality and the gifts that God gave you," said Judge. A thin man with gray hair and an easy smile, he was sixty-eight when he died.

At the Fire Department, where he was known as Father Mike, Judge's parish knew no bounds. He ministered to firefighters and police, but also to crime victims, street youths, and all manner of people who found themselves in crisis. He often took his meals at a firehouse in midtown Manhattan.

"The TWA families considered him a saint," said Hans Ephraimson-Abt, a New Jersey businessman and longtime advocate for families of air crash victims. "He was absolutely hands-on. Religion didn't make any difference for him—he was the same toward everyone, regardless of their beliefs."

Judge helped to organize services on the beach for the Flight 800 families. A news photograph of him at last year's service, wearing his brown robe and gazing out to sea, was distributed around the country. "The water becomes sacred to them," he said of the families.

Judge's funeral drew hundreds of mourners to St. Francis of Assisi Church in midtown Manhattan, including former President Clinton, Sen. Hillary Rodham Clinton, and their daughter, Chelsea. Only a few dozen firefighters were able to attend. Many were still digging through the pile of rubble that used to be the World Trade Center, where scores of their own lie buried.

> American writer Kate Wheeler found herself stranded alone in Shanghai in the aftermath of the attacks. To pass time, she went to a jazz performance at a bar where she met an elderly Japanese school teacher and his former pupil. Upon finding out where she was from, the woman made her an origami crane (a Japanese symbol of peace, which covers the memorial at Hiroshima) and told her how sorry she was. The man requested a song in honor of the U.S.—"Tennessee Waltz." As the Chinese musicians played, the American and the Japanese cried.

CHAINS OF HOPE

Lorri Helfand, *St. Petersburg Times*

*L*ast year, Kennedy Middle School [in St. Petersburg, Florida] planned to make a spirit chain out of strips of construction paper in school colors. But they never finished it, and the paper ended up on a shelf in the back of Judy King's classroom.

After last week's horrific events, students and staffers had a new project in mind for those red, white, and blue pieces of paper.

On Thursday morning, two days after the attacks on New York and Washington, D.C., Kennedy Middle began a chain of hope. In their first period classes, the whole campus wrote messages on the patriotic strips of paper.

The school made the chain "because everybody felt like they needed to do something but weren't sure what it was," said King, who teaches personal development and peer mediation. The goal: "To let (survivors and their families) know that we're behind them."

The idea emerged in a morning staff meeting the day after the attack. Kennedy Middle educators suggested that students write their names on slips of paper and link them together.

Teachers talked it over with their classes, and students had several ideas of their own. They wanted to write personal messages on the paper strips. They wanted to hang the chain of hope in the cafeteria. Eventually, they wanted to send the chain to a New York fire station to share their ideas and encouragement.

Monday morning, students from King's peer mediation class stapled together smaller chains from each class. Then they hung the chain of more than 1,000 messages around the cafeteria, from light fixtures, down the center of the room, and over the water fountain.

"It's going to show people that we do care. It's not just New York. In Florida, people are grieving," said Nathan Wysk, 13, peer mediator and eighth-grader.

Messages in the chain scrawled in pen, pencil and felt tip markers offer words of hope and encouragement, as well as anger:

"I hope we can pull through and rebuild what we lost."

"Dear New York, Don't lose hope. I'm sure some people are still alive."

"I'm sad that people died, and I am very mad that some one would do this."

"I been to the twin tower and I feel sorry and fearful for you guys that are hurt or dead because of it. You will be in our prayers. God bless you all."

There were also desires to return to the days before the attack: "I wish this tragedy wouldn't have happened."

But no matter how her students chose to express themselves, principal Freddie Robinson said she thinks the chain of hope will help them deal with the tragedy. "It gives them a sense of a pride and a sense of hope for all the victims that lost their lives," Robinson said. "It shows everyone that we care about the United States of America."

© *St. Petersburg Times* 2001

> Saade Mustafa is a native New Yorker and Gulf War veteran who is employed as an electrician for the NBC drama *Third Watch*. "My first thought [after hearing of the attacks] was, 'I hope the terrorists are not Arab,'" he says. "I knew there would be backlash." Then he thought, "I am American, 100 percent. I served my country once, and I wanted to serve it again." So he rushed to the site to unload food and set up lights

so rescue workers could work through the night. He did feel self-conscious at the site (only about fifty of New York City's 11,500 firefighters are Muslim), and he cringed when other volunteers called his name. "They were yelling, 'Hey, Saade!' 'Hey, Mustafa!' and I was thinking, 'Call me Moose.' That's what people called me in the service."

Neal C. Lauron/Columbus Post-Dispatch

Gotham's Real Heroes Wear Fire Helmets

Rhonda Chriss Lokeman, *Kansas City Star*

*W*hen I grow up, I want to be a firefighter. I want to rush into buildings on the verge of collapse, where people are hanging for dear life from window ledges and hoping rescuers will see them and bring them safely down. I want to submerge in my subconscious the acrid stench of unidentified dust and melting steel—or worse—as I listen for the tap, tap, tap of fingers beneath rubble telegraphing: "Over here! I'm over here!" And then, when I find a moment to myself, I will collapse in a heap of emotions beneath my helmet, convulse and with dirty hands wipe away my sooty tears.

Then I will return to confront the horrible sight of people with no place to turn except to me. I get no bonuses, no commissions, for each life saved. When I grow up, I want to be a firefighter.

I want to be like Kirk Pritchard. The New York firefighter, along with countless others, risked his life in the rescue effort at the World Trade Center after its twin towers sustained aerial assaults. Armed only with hoses, ladders, and pickaxes, firefighters faced the world's most diabolical foes: terrorists who had hijacked two commercial jets and used them as guided missiles to kill thousands of people.

According to the *New York Times,* Pritchard's spine was fractured after he was hit by falling debris. And yet—and yet—Pritchard managed to walk for hours trying to find others, including fellow firefighters, who were trapped in the tangle of steel and concrete.

He called out to them by name. Some answered. Some didn't.

Whoever said our heroes wear Spandex or have phenomenal batting averages or hawk expensive athletic shoes and make six-figure salaries was wrong.

Heroes look like Pritchard, bald and paralyzed and doped up on painkillers as they try to fathom, between slipping in and out of consciousness, whether they dreamed the whole gawd-awful mess. For Pritchard and others, their constant nightmare is worse than ours. The scenes on television that we can dismiss with a single channel change play over and again in their heads. It is constant and unrelenting. Every sense—sight, taste, smell, touch, and hearing—is hauntingly fine-tuned to September 11.

Our heroes walk into burning buildings and carry out strangers. They never get the key to the city. But they sometimes get the kid hiding in a closet in a bedroom engulfed in flames. Or they get the once-steely office worker who clings fearfully to a handrail on a stairwell blocked by fire and smoke.

Our heroes wear heavy coats, not red capes. They don't leap tall buildings in a single bound; they walk into towering infernos 100-plus stories high. They have singed mustaches and smudged faces. They have meat on their bones, and some have paunch over their belts. Sometimes they drink too much and sleep too little. Our heroes make mistakes. They are not perfect.

When I grow up, I want to be a firefighter.

I want to be like Mike Fitzpatrick. The New York firefighter told reporters about how he and others agonized over the firefighter they had to leave behind. They had just begun to cut him free of the first tower's heap when the second tower showed signs of giving way. They had to leave him. They lost sight of him in the mushroom of dust and smoke that followed. "We were trying to dig him out. We were trying to dig him out," Fitzpatrick repeated, as if trying to reconcile his narrow escape with his conscience.

Our heroes are in constant turmoil about whether they did the right thing, whether they acted quickly enough, whether they could have done more.

When I grow up, I want to be a firefighter, like the ones who worked with Father Mychal Judge. Judge, the New York Fire Department chaplain, was administering last rites to a firefighter trapped by the first tower collapse.

In reverence, Judge removed his fire helmet. Something struck his head and killed him. A small group of firefighters left the scene to carry the monk's lifeless body to a nearby church. They then returned to their weighty task. At Judge's funeral, he was dressed in his brown Franciscan frock. A fire helmet lay beside him in the coffin.

When I grow up, I want to be a firefighter.

A few days after the disaster, several of Manhattan's finest eateries joined together to cook for the rescuers. They used a boat to travel down the Hudson to deliver their five-star meals.

CHAPTER 24

AP/Wide World Photos

DOING THEIR PART

Christina Ward, Staff Writer, *redcross.org*

*O*hio residents Gertrude Zell, eighty-two, and Mildred Roberts, eighty-one, know firsthand how the American Red Cross helps people during times of national crisis. Both women raised young children during World War II, while their husbands fought overseas. Both received Red Cross assistance when times got tough. So in the days following the September 11 attacks, Gertrude and Mildred wanted to do their part for the Red Cross. Along with a team of other Rest Haven Nursing Home residents and workers in the small town of Greenville, they came up with a modest money-raising plan—a plan that quickly grew beyond expectations.

It started out with a simple act of patriotism. Shortly after the disaster, a staff member at Rest Haven suggested that residents create their own American flag pins to wear and show support. "We all liked that idea, and then someone said, 'Why don't we sell them, and give the money to the Red Cross relief effort?'" Gertrude recalled. "So we got to work!"

"We all just wanted to find a way to help during this awful time," Mildred added.

Four of the residents began creating small pins with cut-out paper flags, pin backs, and ribbons. Pricing the pins at $1 each, they offered them initially to other residents, staff, and visitors. The goal was to make $100 by the end of the week. Gertrude went so far as to sit by the front door of Rest Haven, in her wheelchair, and speak to everyone who walked in. Her sales pitch was a hit.

"That first day, they made $97," said Corinna Alexander, a floor supervisor at Rest Haven. "So they increased the goal to $150. By the next afternoon, they'd already raised $250, and there were more orders coming in."

Word spread throughout the surrounding community, and local media outlets soon picked up on the project. Boosted by newspaper articles, radio reports, and a visit from a local TV station, demand soared. Businesses and residents wanted to buy the flag pins to distribute to their employees and neighbors. Local office workers were stopping by, buying pins to take back to friends and family. It became clear that four pinmakers couldn't handle the volume, and family members and other volunteers pitched in to help the senior citizens with their project.

As of this writing, the pin sale had raised more than $4,000—and orders are still rolling in. "The fundraising goal has gone up and up, with each day," Corinna said, laughing. "Now the ladies are hoping to make $5,000—I think it's a pretty safe bet they'll hit that!"

Gertrude and Mildred admitted that after days of pinmaking, they were getting a little tired. But they remained determined, with plans to continue until the last order comes in. The nation's current crisis reminds them of World War II and the dedication it inspired in average citizens.

"The desecration of our beautiful country is just horrible," Mildred said, choking up. "We all have to do what we can to help those families affected by this." She recalled the time, years ago, when the Red Cross assisted her family. "In 1944, my husband had just left to go overseas, and I went into labor. I wasn't quite sure where they had sent him. The Red Cross tracked him down, though, and gave him the message: He had a beautiful new baby boy."

Gertrude told a similar story. "My husband was in the service during the war, flying planes in the South Pacific," she said. "One day I was robbed—all my money was stolen, and I didn't have cash to buy food for my children. The Red Cross gave me money until my husband's pay came through."

Both women said the pin project has been a wonderful experience, despite the long hours. But they add that the difficult circumstances make it hard, sometimes.

"We've had a lot of fun making the flags. We've laughed a lot during those hours," Gertrude said. "But we've cried a lot, too. This is a very sad time for the country."

Actress Kathleen Turner wanted to do her part. So she volunteered as a dispatcher at St. Vincent's Hospital in New York, where she made sure supplies got to the proper departments.

How Kids Can Help

Karen Fanning, Scholastic

*T*he suffering of thousands of families who lost loved ones in the deadliest terrorist attack in U.S. history won't easily be erased. But kids can show their support by lending a helping hand, even if they live thousands of miles from "Ground Zero." Here are some ways to pitch in:

- If you are seventeen or older and weigh at least 110 pounds, you can donate blood at your local American Red Cross chapter. Log on to *www.helping.org* to locate the chapter nearest you.

- Organize an event, such as a bake sale or car wash, at your school to raise money for surviving family members. Well-known charities, such as the United Way and the American National Red Cross, have set up special relief funds to aid surviving family members of the World Trade Center disaster. To learn how you can donate money, tools, and supplies to these and other organizations, log on to *www.helping.org*.

- E-mail President Bush and your local state representatives with your thoughts about how the United States should respond to the terrorist acts. Log on to *www.youthnoise.com*.

- You can also make lapel pins with red, white, and blue ribbons to hand out to friends and family. Your entire class can make the pins to give to other classes to wear in support of America. You can use three-color ribbon, or a strip of each color. Twist them together and either pin or staple them into a loop. The loops pin easily to lapels with safety pins and are a good way to show your patriotism.

- If you'd like to express your sorrow to the many kids who've lost family members, you can create artwork and send it to: YouthNOISE, 2000 M Street, NW, Suite 500, Washington, DC 20036.

Silvion Ramsundar was on the 78th floor of the South Tower when the plane crashed into the building. Bleeding badly from the chest, he somehow made it to the 50th floor. There he encountered Douglas Brown, who stopped the bleeding and led him down the flights of stairs and out to a medic. Rushed to the hospital, he survived.

AN ALL TOO
EXPERIENCED VOICE

A commercial jet exploding in a terrorist attack was nothing new to Helen Engelhardt. Thirteen years before the World Trade Center towers collapsed, in December 1988, Helen's husband had been blown out of the sky over Lockerbie, Scotland, as a passenger aboard Pan Am flight 103.

Helen was left behind to raise their six-year-old son, Alan. Tony Hawkins had gone to England for a week to visit an uncle who was dying of cancer and to take care of family business. He was supposed to return December 20 but called to say things were going slower than he expected and he wanted to stay an extra day.

"Well, of course, one more day was okay," Helen said. "How could I say no to that?" The only flight available December 21 was 103, and he booked his seat. "As my son said for a couple of years, 'Why didn't you say no?' Well, I didn't say no because I didn't know to say no. I know that, but I also know that if I had said no, he'd be alive, and that's a particular anguish that's there that can't go away."

Helen was waiting up with Alan for Tony's return when she got a phone call from his cousin in England. The plane had exploded at 30,000 feet. The only hope was that Tony might have missed the flight. Helen told Alan the plane had a mechanical delay and wouldn't be back until the next day.

"I had to protect my child first, and so I made up a story to protect him until I got more information . . . so that he could go to bed and I could find out what happened," Helen said. "He collapsed immediately—all the fatigue that he was holding back waiting to see Daddy."

As hours passed and Tony didn't call, Helen realized she was connected to a vast tragedy. "I didn't know quite yet how many people had died and who they were, but I wasn't alone. This just hadn't happened to my husband," she said. As friends gathered the next day, she packed Alan off to a neighbor's house with instructions that they shield him from any media or discussion of the flight. When Alan returned that night to a house full of people but no Daddy, a delegation of Helen's supporters cornered her and demanded that she talk to her son.

"I had already experienced telling a lot of people, and every time I told them Tony died, Tony was alive in their minds until I said he wasn't. And I didn't want to kill Alan's father, which is what I was going to do," Helen said.

She told Alan that his father had died, and she took him to a Mass at St. Patrick's Cathedral, where he saw hundreds of other people affected by the bombing. "I brought my child to see that he wasn't the only child who had lost a parent," she said.

In those early weeks, Helen bonded with other families touched by the Pan Am attack. "I was immediately connected to other people and a group that began to form, and we began putting together our own bereavement group, this other widow and myself," Helen said. It grew into an organization with committees, officers, and a newsletter. "For those of us who wanted to, who needed to channel their anger, this was the vehicle that we created within a month. And I've been there ever since in one degree or another. I've been involved in bereavement counseling, and I've been involved in political work."

Helen's fiftieth birthday fell just a year after Tony's death, and she was unwilling to celebrate with much beyond a small dinner party. But when her sixtieth rolled around, just weeks before the millennium, she was ready to party, to celebrate her rebuilt life. Her cousin asked where. "I immediately said Windows on the World, at the top of the World Trade Center, which I had never been to. I said it because the only place I could think of that was appropriate for a party would be one where I would feel literally on top of the world, and I could take my friends there to be on top of the world."

Helen began working on plans with Jackie Sayegh, a caterer at the restaurant. For months, the two discussed menus, drinks, and room selection. Helen made a trip to Lower Manhattan to photograph the building and the views from on high to include in her invitations. The preparations culminated in the party of a lifetime, with her son, Alan, as the master of ceremonies.

Almost two years later, on September 11, Helen was on the phone making plans to fly to Tennessee for a storytelling festival when a neighbor, who was working on her basement, walked upstairs with a quizzical look on his face. His wife had just called his cell phone to tell him about the World Trade Center attack.

At first, she didn't make any personal connections to the World Trade Center. "All that day when I rushed downtown to try to give blood, to try to offer sanctuary to anyone stranded in the Marriott Hotel who wanted to come back to my house to spend the night, I wasn't thinking about Windows on the World or the people who were working there that morning. Three days later, I suddenly started thinking about Jackie and the others."

Helen tracked down Jackie's phone number and called her home. "A woman answered the phone, so I thought for a second she was safe, that she hadn't been at work, but it was her aunt." Jackie had called relatives a few minutes after the plane struck her tower below her. She hadn't been heard from since. When Helen learned of a memorial service for Jackie, she contacted the family.

"I called her aunt to say that I could not come; I was going to a meeting of the families of Pan Am 103, and I let her know my connection," Helen said. She also asked for the address of Jackie's parents, and she sent a letter to them and to those who had attended her party, in case they hadn't realized their ties to someone in the building.

Helen's letter to Jackie's parents, reads, in part:

I'm writing to tell you of my profound sorrow and regret that
your daughter Jackie was a victim of the terrible attack on the
World Trade Center. I met Jackie two years ago, when I decided to
celebrate my 60th birthday by giving myself a spectacular party....
From early September, when I first made contact with her and we
chose the date, till the night itself, December 4, Jackie and I worked
closely together planning every detail of the event....

Jackie was thoughtful and meticulous with details, ready to
modify plans as I told her to....The party was everything I wanted
it to be; even the weather cooperated and was clear and mild. Every
detail contributed to its success; my friends still talk about it as the
most memorable party they have ever gone to.

It could never have happened without Jackie. I was hoping
against hope that she didn't go to work that morning or was
somehow delayed in getting there.

There is a lovely saying in the Jewish faith about someone who
has died, "May their memory be for a blessing." Jackie's memory is a
blessing.

Among the topics Helen's group, Victims of Pan Am Flight 103, has tack-
led is airport security. She is outraged that the September 11 attack could
have taken place against the backdrop of Pan Am 103 and the lessons learned
there. And yet she sees great hope in what her group can offer in immediate,
personal ways. At the Saturday meeting that coincided with Jackie's memorial service, group members discussed opening the ranks to include people
touched by the latest attacks—not just as welcome visitors, but as members—so they wouldn't have to reinvent the wheel.

"What we know better than anybody else is how to help the newly
bereaved, and there are thousands of them," Helen said. "We know, and we

can get to a level immediately with a total stranger that you can't with anybody else.

"Mental health professionals should be optimistic. They should help people understand that they can survive, and flourish even, and grow. I'm not a survivor; I'm a different person. I'm full of energy, and I'm full of *joix de vivre*. I'm not in a puddle on the floor. The excruciating pain and confusion will not last forever, and you can find your way out of it and make a new life for yourself. That is possible....

"We can offer this, and we want to."

> Petrit Mahmuti of Pristina, Kosovo, who had flown into Washington for a short vacation three days before the quadruple airline crashes, said that he walked for hours that Wednesday and Thursday, searching for the Red Cross, so that he too could donate blood. "In my country, we have been under war attacks and terrorist conditions for more than ten years, and aid from the Red Cross—food, clothes, and medicine—was very important in our neighborhoods," he said. "I understand how Americans feel at this moment. It is my honor to be here at the Red Cross now. It is not very much, but I want to give a little bit of my health to the American people."

CHAPTER 27

Stacia Philips Deshishku

REACHING OUT SPIRITUALLY

Alexa Capeloto and Sheryl James, *Detroit Free Press*

September 24, 2001: For two hours Sunday, a downtown Detroit sanctuary represented church, mosque, temple and synagogue for worshipers of all faiths to pray to their common God for peace in the wake of the Sept. 11 terrorist attacks.

Fort Street Presbyterian Church hosted leaders of various faiths and hundreds of their followers for perhaps the largest local interfaith service since the attacks. The sanctuary, with seating for 1,200 people, was packed with worshipers and lined with the flags of numerous nations.

The service ended a day of worship that began with a special mass at Holy Redeemer Catholic Church in Detroit, where fallen New York firefighters and police officers were honored by metro Detroit comrades.

At Fort Street Presbyterian, leaders and attendees sang, prayed and spoke in the name of peace.

John Murphy, 71, cried as the Detroit 300 tricentennial choir—reassembled for the special service—sang out, "Open the eyes of my heart, Lord/I want to see you."

"We've got to get through this somehow," said Murphy, a Detroit resident, as he stood with his wife, Virginia. "It's too big for me right now. It overwhelms me, what those people did to us."

The voices of choir members filled the church, bringing people to their feet, their hands clapping and bodies swaying. A small United States flag stuck out from one pew.

The service was evidence of the strong interfaith ties cultivated in metro Detroit over the years. Muslim, Jewish and Christian leaders sat side by side in the pews and behind the pulpit, taking turns in prayer and reflection.

Detroit Catholic Cardinal Adam Maida asked for justice, not vindictiveness, in the country's retaliatory efforts.

He also prayed for families of men and women in the armed forces who are being called up for duty.

Al Fishman, a member of the Peace Action Committee of Michigan, was there to echo Maida's concerns about any future war waged by the United States.

"This is a time to ensure that our nation doesn't become a mirror image of the terrorists that inflicted this terrible tragedy on our nation," Fishman said, standing at the door of the sanctuary.

The theme of the Fort Street Presbyterian service appeared to be hope, while respect and grief shaped morning mass at Holy Redeemer. About 30 members of the Detroit Fire Department filled the front pews, joining regular worshipers to honor their comrades in New York.

As firefighters prayed inside the church, an American flag fluttered outside, held about 35 feet in the air between two raised fire engine ladders. U.S. flags also draped the fire trucks.

"We were just happy to do something for our brothers in New York," said Louis Gusoff, battalion chief of Ladder No. 8, the 99-year-old fire station two blocks down Junction Avenue from Holy Redeemer.

Several firefighters gathering before the service praised the generosity of residents of the area, which is a center of Detroit's Hispanic community. Four days of fire-boot collections taken at neighborhood intersections last week netted $28,000, Gusoff said.

"Our eyes were watering the whole time we were passing the boot," said Capt. Ron Winchester.

Citywide, firefighters had collected $297,246 as of Sunday, Gusoff said.

The Rev. Don Hanchon, pastor of Holy Redeemer, said the congregation contributed $3,000 in a special collection last week.

"I don't have the magic answer as to why this tragedy happened," Han-chon told his congregation Sunday.

But, he said, the firefighters, police officers and emergency services personnel who responded in New York were "the answer to a prayer."

Firefighters in communities around the United States traditionally do boot collections, where they put out fire boots to be filled with donations. But no one has ever seen the outpouring of contributions like those that occurred in the wake of the attacks. Here are some on-line postings reporting the contributions:

"Our county raised over $500,000 in twelve hours."

"We raised over $18,000 [in one day]. I have never seen such generosity from the public. And this was one department within my town. I know others had equal or greater success."

"Sixty firefighters, cops, and medical types fanned out over the 32 square miles of my town and collected $99,974 in 5 hours."

"Some woman gave us a $2,000 check. One guy gave $5 then asked what it was for. When the chief told him he wanted the $5 back. Then he threw in a ten. People were thanking us for standing out there.... Wait ... aren't they the ones helping us help our fallen brothers? I had chills all day long and not because I was cold."

Tim Schulteis

A MODICUM OF COMFORT

Caren Messing

*T*hrough the owner of the Swedish Institute for Massage Therapy, two colleagues and I were dispatched one day after the attacks to an undisclosed New York location to massage the bereaving families of missing NYPD and rescue workers. With no guarantee we'd make it through the labyrinth of checkpoints, we managed to park the car a block north of Chambers on the West Side Highway. We had no idea if the car would be there at the end of the day, or even accessible—due to all the buses shuttling workers into the site and flat-bed trucks lined up ready to cargo away the tortuous remnants of the World Trade Center. It took almost an hour to pass through the final checkpoint with the Army and receive the red laminated "NYC Disaster Relief" passes for secure admittance.

We met with an NYPD sergeant, who drove us to Police Headquarters, where we were to work in the auditorium. On the way, the sergeant told us that it had been an emotional day—they had found a pocket of 400 bodies, and the mission had transformed from "rescue" to "recovery."

I worked on a woman who's missing her two sons: one a fireman and the other a police officer. I worked on an officer who had just come from the site. He laid down, gun and all, and began making small talk. At one point he said, "Gee, I haven't had one of these massages since Oklahoma." I didn't get it at first. . . . The Broadway show? . . . Then I realized—this is a whole different world.

After the shift, the sergeant took me and one of my co-workers to the actual site. As we walked along the restricted zone, wearing hard hats and masks among the firefighters, ironworkers and NYPD, the scene seemed to be in slow motion: The fetid smell. The paste underfoot. Searching eye glances; mutual acknowledgment of what cannot be put into words. Surrendering. Unraveling. Stepping through a landscape of shared awareness of our thinly veiled mortality. I am being led. Do I know to where I walk? I've been here before. Have I been here before?

We walked further through. The nighttime stadium floodlights displacing stark reality into further sharp contrasts of light and dark—unreality. The nullity of memory—I am here right now I am here right now right now right now. This is happening.

The hardest thing was leaving. . . . My heart still is tearing—how can I leave? I can not leave; I must help.

> Julia DeVita is nine years old. Her cousin is missing in the World Trade Center rubble. The Charlotte, North Carolina, resident wanted to do something—so she and friends decided to give their profits from their drink and cookies stand to relief efforts. In three days they raised nearly $1,500—this from a business that usually nets around $8 a weekend. "We wish we could make a $10 million donation like Bill Gates," says Julia. "But we're doing what we can."

Stacia Philips Deshishku

ON THE OTHER SIDE OF THE WORLD

From *redcross.org* and other sources

*A*s Americans try to return to their normal lives amid fears of more terrorist attacks, thousands of relief workers are trying to offer aid to millions of Afghani refugees. Over the past twenty years, millions of Afghans have fled drought and war. Inside Afghanistan, the Afghan Red Crescent is trying to tend to both groups, but the magnitude of the humanitarian crisis is too much for it to handle alone. The Pakistan and Iran Red Crescent societies also are trying to deal with a refugee population that could grow to epic proportions. As of October 2001, the two bordering nations already were home to almost 4 million Afghan refugees.

In addition, before the current situation, the UN estimates that more than 5 million of the country's 26 million people depend on international aid to survive. The International Federation of the Red Cross has launched an appeal for nearly $5.5 million to assist 300,000 people in need of shelter, health care, clean water, and food.

Around the world, Red Cross societies are reaching out to help in other ways. "The response worldwide to our appeal has been very impressive," said Jean Ayoub, operations director for the Federation. "In 48 hours we have received pledges of 6 million Swiss francs in assistance from the Red Cross and Red Crescent in America, Austria, Belgium, Britain, Finland, France, Netherlands, Norway, Saudi Arabia, Sweden, the United Arab Emirates, Japan, and Switzerland. This will allow us to start airlifting medical supplies into Pakistan in the next days and to purchase significant quantities of relief locally. We are also boosting the resources of our member Red Crescent Societies in Iran, Tajikistan, Uzbekistan, and Turkmenistan."

As of this writing, President Bush has committed $320 million in aid to the plight of the Afghanis, including $25 million in emergency aid that will go to the United Nations, the Red Cross, and other groups providing food and medicine to the Afghans and Afghani refugees.

In the days following the attack, Kerry McGinnis, a kennel manager for Manhattan's Humane Society, rescued more than 200 pets from apartments near Ground Zero.

CHAPTER 30

Kim Sparks

NO TERRORISTS ON THIS PLAYGROUND!

Ms. Mac

*W*hen I received the phone call that the World Trade Center had been hit, I was in the classroom and my students were quietly working on their math. As the details were described to me over the phone, the innocence of the young children in front of me remained intact. Knowing that visuals can impact a child in more ways than one, I knew better than to turn on the television. My stomach churned, but at the same time I felt unusually calm. My serenity was not blatant disrespect for all those who were directly involved while I was so far away, but rather from my belief that goodness would have to come out of this.

I knew that the line had been drawn. I knew now that our country, which for the past few years has debated in circles the nuances of the definitions of truth/dishonesty, honor/dishonor, guilt/innocence, would now have a clear definition of something. We could now clearly say that this action was unequivocally wrong. Values would have to return to our country—compassion, loyalty, honor, dedication, empathy, tenacity, patriotism.

I quietly asked the children if they would like an early recess, and with a resounding Yes, we went outside. Watching them, I realized that in front of my eyes were the most ethnically diverse group of children I have ever taught. Before me were children of Venezuelan, Filipino, English, Scottish, Lebanese, Hispanic, Honduran, Persian, Native American, Irish, Swiss, Jewish, and German descent. Differences were the catalyst for the horrendous attack, and yet here the differences in front of me were the beauty of the moment.

On the hill of sand in the middle of the yard, an altercation was in progress. Digging vigorously, a would-be archeologist made the mistake of slinging sand over his shoulder right into the face of another student. I started to speak and then held my tongue. Instead of the usual accusations and denials and little feet running to me to report, I witnessed what I hoped would some day be the scene on the international playground. The offender apologized. The victim stood calmly still while appraising the situation, not immediately retaliating. The neighboring entities ran to aid the victim and reprimand the offender. After a while they accepted the offender's apology, sat down, and began again working together for a common goal.

A feeling of peace came over me.

Hatred is taught. How dare the people who hurt innocent people try to teach us to hate! How dare they try to take away the power of the innocent . . . the purity of the soul . . . and the blessing of God . . . our children!

Back into the classroom we marched. I knew I had to prepare these children for what they were surely to hear about later that day. I sat down and made up a story about me hurting the country of Africa (a continent we were studying). Africa was now mad at me and wanted to hurt the United States back because of my stupid mistake. I asked who could fix my mistake. Immediately a six-year-old said, "The President of the United States!"

"How do I know that the president will do a good job?" I asked. "What if he doesn't know what to do?"

"God will tell him what to do," answered another insightful child.

I finally revealed in limited detail that our country had been hurt and that the president, as well as the victims and their children, needed our help. Out of the mouths of these babes came a solution. "We can send him our money," suggested a seven-year-old.

With the help of parents, community leaders, and a field trip to the local bank, these small sandlot diplomats put their collection of various coins and dollars on the table. They signed on the dotted line. They gave their money to help the president by buying U.S. Savings Bonds. Some promised to hold onto the bonds for their own future educational needs, promising to learn more to help others. Others pledged to send the money to the children of the victims when President Bush is finished "borrowing" their money.

"There!" said one small but powerful voice. "That should scare the bad guys!"

> Ms. Mac teaches at Horizons Academy, a one-room learning lab for children in pre-kindergarten through sixth grade in San Angelo, Texas. About thirty of her current and former students bought $50 savings bonds through San Angelo National Bank.

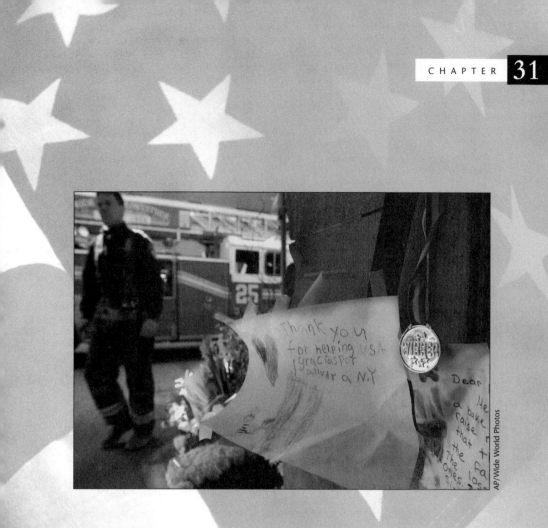

SMALL IS BEAUTIFUL

Andrea Scott, *Idaho Press-Tribune*

*S*trength cannot be measured in numbers. Seven people gathered recently in Caldwell, Idaho's Pioneer Plaza and quietly but passionately remembered those stricken by the September 11 terrorist attacks in New York City and Washington. "This was not meant to be a huge gathering," organizer Lucinda Tyler of Caldwell said. "We just wanted to come together and show our support."

The small park is tucked between a parking lot and the creek that winds through the heart of Caldwell. It is a park designed around a military theme. Inscribed bricks honor four Medal of Honor recipients and other men and women who have served our country. A flag in one corner rises above the plaza, and at its base an inscribed dedication plaque honors Herbert Littleton, a former marine and Medal of Honor winner who once saved eight men from death.

Officially the park is named Littleton Plaza, but many people refer to it as Pioneer Plaza. It is also called Leo's Park by some, after Leo Holmes, the man who has dedicated his life to caring for it. On any given day Leo can be found picking up trash or weeding. "This is a sacred place," Leo Holmes said, his voice tightening with emotion. "It honors our military heritage; it honors our veterans."

Arlene Burdick attended the gathering, and said she has been touched by all the people coming together in the community and the reader boards on the boulevard that show strength and support for our country. "This is about American unity," Caldwell City Councilman Mike Gable said. "Last week's attack on America wasn't a film; there were no special affects—it was real and someone has actually done this to our country."

As the rally came to a close, people shared good-byes and a few smiles as they parted. Many passed a white post rising up out of the park with inscriptions that seemed even more meaningful during these times: "May Peace Prevail on Earth, May Peace Be in Our Homes and Communities."

> Tom Burnett, Mark Bingham, and Jeremy Glick—passengers on flight 93—called their loved ones from the plane to let them know how much they loved them and that they were planning to resist the terrorists who had hijacked their plane.

CHAPTER 32

Drew Kisela

IN MEMORY, WITH LOVE

Kaitlin Kisela

Kaitlin Kisela had flown from Washington Dulles International Airport to Los Angeles on American Airlines flight 77 countless times. Her sister was in school at the University of Southern California and planning her wedding. Kaitlin, fifteen, was to be the maid of honor.

Kaitlin's mother, Panda's, job as a flight attendant on American Airlines had its travel perks, and Kaitlin often made long weekends of trips to Los Angeles with her mom. If Panda took the 3 P.M. out of Dulles on Fridays, Kaitlin would finish school, catch the 6 P.M. flight, and ride with the crew from the airport to the hotel to catch up with her mom. As the wedding plans evolved, the three Kiselas scouted for dresses and made party plans, and then Panda and Kaitlin headed back to their Virginia home.

Kaitlin was in history class September 11 when her teacher turned on a television set.

"It was just after the first plane had hit the first World Trade Center tower," Kaitlin said. "We saw the other one hit the other tower, the other plane. You could tell it was commercial, but I didn't realize it was American. After they said American, I kind of got a little scared, but didn't think much of it because it was out of New York. I thought, 'At least I'm not going to know anybody.'"

About 45 minutes later, Kaitlin heard that flight 77 was missing. "As soon as I heard that, I flipped out, and called my mom. She actually hadn't even heard the rumor that 77 was missing, so I was the one who told her. And then I wanted to go home, and so I just found one of my friends and made him drive me home."

At that moment, Kaitlin became a key pillar in her mom's support system. "I was already crying. My mom was hysterical. The phone was ringing off the hook. We must have gotten at least two to three hundred phone calls." Quickly Panda became part of a network of flight attendants and crew members frantically calling each other to see who was home. "As they were doing this, they kept finding out more and more people were on this flight," Kaitlin said. Panda had flown for more than thirty years, and this was her regular route. Her co-workers were among her closest friends. Kaitlin knew eight people aboard flight 77 that day—all four flight attendants, the pilot, the co-pilot, and two passengers. Panda knew three more passengers beyond those.

Kaitlin wouldn't leave the house for a week. "My friends would just keep coming over because I didn't want to leave my mom. My dad was stuck in Las Vegas till that Saturday. So it was just me and my mom. And I knew that she needed somebody because she was feeling ten times worse than I was, and I didn't want to leave her by herself."

That Wednesday night, Panda tried to persuade Kaitlin to go with her to a church service for people affected by Tuesday's events. "I didn't want to see all my mom's friends. I wasn't ready to, because I knew they were all going to be the way my mom was acting times however many were there. I didn't really want to be there."

So she stayed home and turned inward. "I just sat at the computer and started to write because I normally write if I'm sad. I try to put it in words to make myself feel better." She didn't think she'd done a particularly good job, though. "I printed it out, and just set it on the kitchen table or counter and didn't even really think anything of it."

Kaitlin went to bed; her mom got home late. The next day at school, Kaitlin's counselor called her to the office to take a phone call from her mom. Her mom had found the poem and was stunned. "She couldn't believe that I had written it and I hadn't shown it to her, and she was really touched by it." By that time, her mom had already shared it with other American

Airlines crew members who had gathered at a local hotel to talk. She had read it to friends in San Francisco and Los Angeles.

"People made copies of it. It was already being passed around. I didn't really know how to react to it because, when I had written it, I hadn't thought that it would have an impact. I just wrote it to make myself feel better and to help my mom. I honestly had no idea it would have such an impact. I still think it's kind of weird."

The chief of pilots for American Airlines, thinking that Panda's older daughter in California had written it and would be unavailable, called Panda to ask whether she would read the poem at the memorial service for American Airline employees who had been based in the area. Panda didn't think she could get through it.

Kaitlin stepped in. She read her poem before about 1,500 people at an Alexandria, Virginia, hotel. When she began to choke up, she glanced at a friend of her mom's, whose smile urged her on. In the days afterward, Kaitlin received thank-you cards and phone calls, many from people she'd never met. "I didn't really expect anything to come out of it, but I'm happy that it could help people."

In Memory, With Love

Times of laughter, now times of tears
Times of joy, now times of fears

Smiling faces, now out of sight
Vengeful enemies, now filled with delight

Questions unanswered we hear people call
Surreal events that have happened to us all

But times of unity have now begun
For these monsters must know that they have not yet won

Although tragic events have caused loved ones to part
They live on strongly in our memories and our hearts

Throughout all the heartache and anger we feel
These innocent souls will help us deal

Listen to their whispers and you will hear
A message that will come loud and clear

These heroes will never be entirely gone
In our familiar skies their spirits forever live on

For what this sadness and grief undoubtedly brings
Are several new angels to sit on our wings.

9-12-01

At one Fill-the-Boot firefighter fundraising campaign, the fast food chain Wendy's let the firefighters put their fire truck in the Wendy's lot, changed their sign to support the Fill-the-Boot campaign, and gave them free sodas and water all day long.

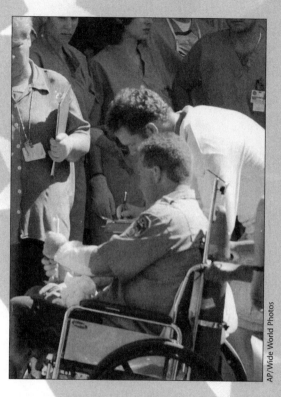

CHAPTER 33

AP/Wide World Photos

"I NEED TO BE THERE"

Aaron Kuriloff, *Times-Picayune*

September 18, 2001: Like doctors throughout New York City, Jeff Dongieux, a New Orleans native doing his medical residency at Bellevue Hospital, rushed to Ground Zero in the aftermath of the terrorist attacks on the World Trade Center towers. He expected his colleagues would treat hundreds of wounded people, perhaps thousands.

The full magnitude of Tuesday's horror has been driven home to him by a single fact: There have been scarcely any survivors to treat.

Dongieux is part of a rotating pool of doctors authorized to aid relief workers and victims at the site of the devastation. The pile of smoking rubble covers an area the size of the Superdome and the New Orleans Arena combined, with some sections jutting ten stories in the air. The surrounding field of ash and debris is the size of the French Quarter, said Dongieux, who grew up near Audubon Park and studied oral and facial surgery at LSU School of Medicine.

He spends most of his time at Ground Zero in a ruined World Trade Center mini-mart that functions as a triage center. There he treats not the rescued but the rescuers: a firefighter struck by falling glass, a National Guardsman who has twisted an ankle working in the rubble. Almost everybody suffers from respiratory problems amid the unrelenting smoke and ash. "I wish I could tell you I'd resuscitated twenty people. But when you see how those buildings came down, well, it would have taken a miracle for anyone to survive that," he said.

Dongieux instead heals anyone he can, providing a suture here and eye drops there, then moves on to Bellevue, and stays up all night treating his regular patients.

Through it all, he bears witness.

"It smells like rotten milk," he said. "When I first got down there, I was wondering if I'd walked into a store where milk had gone bad. But everywhere I went, I could still smell it. It's decay."

What he found was a scene evocative of Dresden after that German city was firebombed in World War II. "It looked almost like a volcanic eruption," he said. "There was soot and ash all over the place.

For almost half an hour, Dongieux stood in the plaza, aghast, unable to move. Firefighters raced past, dragging hoses over shattered computers, filing cabinets, and charred mounds of paper, but for Dongieux, there was no one to treat. Finally, a nurse and an emergency medical technician brought him to One Liberty Plaza, where he found other residents from Bellevue setting up IV stations and oxygen tanks. Some firefighters were sleeping in a row of bunks, while about fifty others lined up to have soot removed from their eyes.

At 2:30 A.M., Dongieux walked down stuck escalators and over a carpet of glass shards to use the bathroom in the subway station at Chambers Street and One Liberty Place. Inside, he said, was a second level of destruction. "Where the entrance should have been to the subway stop, all the iron stuff had collapsed in on itself," he said. "It was crazy. You could just visualize what had happened. Time was captured right there."

Two hours later, soot-blackened and still sleepless, he was back at Bellevue to begin a 4:30 A.M. shift that did not end for twelve hours. Upon returning to Ground Zero, he found his post had been evacuated. The building he had occupied the night before was in danger of collapsing. He turned around and headed home.

A day or two later, emergency workers called him back and he resumed work in the mini-mart. "Mostly it's just people coming in for little bitty things," he said. "Minor lacerations. Eye baths. They paged me at 6 A.M. because a National Guard guy got hit in the face and they thought he might have a fracture, but they treated him at a military facility."

He expects to serve one or two nights a week until the digging ends. The site is now organized into piles, with dump trucks carrying loads out of the way every few minutes. Yet as the cleanup continues, the work gets grimmer. And even though he spends most of his time carrying water or supplies, and running errands for the work crews, he's happy to stay all night. "This is something bigger than anything we've ever seen," he said. "I need to be there."

Army health policy officer Lt. Col. Patty Horoho was in the Pentagon when it was hit. She set up a triage center and treated more than seventy-five people, at first with only a first-aid kit, before EMT workers began to arrive.

CHAPTER 34

"The Love Is the Best Thing"

Lora Volkert, *Idaho Press-Tribune*

*T*hey're Bosnians, Vietnamese, and Peruvians no more. They're American citizens now. And at no better time. On Monday September 17, 2001, ninety-two applicants from thirty-four countries became naturalized American citizens at a ceremony in the Nampa, Idaho, Civic Center. While the terrorist attacks on the World Trade Center and Pentagon tinged the event with sadness, the tragedies in no way dimmed the new citizens' pride. As she was helped across the stage, an eighty-two-year-old Iranian woman clutched her miniature U.S. flag high above her head. A Mexican woman expecting a baby was given two flags with her citizenship papers. In an especially moving moment, ninety-two new citizens and their friends and families rose to sing "The Star-Spangled Banner."

Many of the new citizens expressed sadness about last week's tragedy. However, Dolly Janeth Quast, originally from Colombia, said that while she was sad for those who lost their lives, she only felt the strength of her patriotism grow. "My heart is very strong," Quast said. "I want to be a better citizen, especially because of the tragedy and for the people that suffer." Marcella Hurtado-Gomez admitted to mixed feelings of joy and trepidation on the heels of last week's deadly violence. She said the attacks were "a little scary," but even though they haven't had much time to sink in, they haven't changed her gratitude and pride.

Muhamed Prcic, a native of Bosnia-Herzegovina, had an unswerving thought: "I am very proud to become United States citizen—very happy now." But he shared the same shocked feelings about last week's attacks with millions of his fellow American citizens. "I am very sad about New York," Prcic said. "Just hope that it never happens again." Prcic, along with Rudolf and Enisa Jozelic, also of Bosnia-Herzegovina, have lived in the United States for almost eight years. Rudolf Jozelic said he only felt excitement and pride. "It's really a proud time—a proud time to become a citizen right now. What else to say? Whatever you say is not enough."

Some of the new citizens said they felt embraced by other Americans, even at a difficult time. "I like people here," said Gurmit Kaur Sandhu, originally of India. "They're very nice to me. I'm happy." As for the attacks, Sandhu said, "It doesn't matter. I will live here. I'm not afraid of the terrorism. Terrorism can happen in any country." She continued with a call for peace and understanding. "I send my good wishes for the American people. I think we should learn to treat everybody as brothers and sisters. That will help to bring us close—if we know each other, if we all love each other. The love is the best thing."

Thirty-two-year-old Nicole Blackman spent days after the attacks serving coffee and kind words to emergency crews in New York. One man, as he departed with a steaming cup, turned to his co-worker exclaiming, "She's like from another planet: home."

CHAPTER 35

Michael Macor *San Francisco Chronicle*

THE BOOKSTORE ANGEL

Eric Brazil, *San Francisco Chronicle*

*T*hey're calling Catherine Bohne "The Angel of Park Slope." In the hours after the September 11 attack, Bohne transformed the Brooklyn's Community Bookstore, which she owns, into her neighborhood's disaster-relief center.

The collapse of the World Trade Center towers in Lower Manhattan set off an instant need for such things as food, bedding, housing, information—and an outlet for New Yorkers who wanted, somehow, to help the victims.

The bookstore, at 143 Seventh Street, filled that need, and Bohne still sounds amazed in describing how it evolved, starting with the simple posting of a notice on the store's window asking for blood donations.

She cleared out the center of the bookstore, which soon was piled high with clothing, food, and bedding—and the phones were ringing off the hook. Volunteers appeared by the dozen, including some who had lost family members.

"One lady brought in some sheets, and she said, 'These are the sheets my husband slept on his last night,'" Bohne said.

She was "just a bookstore clerk" before the emergency, Bohne said, but quickly found herself in charge of what became a citywide relief operation.

"She has a natural talent for it," said Sarah Sills, a freelance graphic designer who helped coordinate the effort after stopping by the bookstore to deliver some dog food. "She's just been an angel to the neighborhood, providing a place where people could come and really do something." Everyone who came to check the store window "was dying to help," Bohne said. "I'd say something like, 'If you want to help, go out and buy some cooked chickens'—and they would," she said.

Bohne, thirty-three, who studied for a year in Swaziland as a teenager before returning to the United States to finish college, said the Park Slope community was so eager to help that the simple posting of the note on the bookstore window had generated a huge response.

Real estate agents who serve the area that is bounded by Prospect Park and Flatbush and 15th Avenues offered housing, and nearly 100 restaurants provided hot food for relief workers, while residents brought in dozens of cooked chickens, pots of homemade soup, bread, and salads.

Two nights after the attack, relief workers at Stuyvesant High School near the World Trade Center called to say they were living off Power Bars and Gatorade and feeling horrible. They asked, 'Could you get us green salad and some hot chicken?'" she said.

When Greg Gallagher, a third-grade teacher at Park Slope's P.S. 321, delivered the food, firefighters and other relief workers lined up, and every one of them shook his hand, Bohne said.

Michelle Valladares, who runs a Buddhist center in Manhattan, called the bookstore owner "a heroine. She is truly unbelievable. She ran barefoot through the street to help people. She found out what people needed and what to do about it. On the night of the 11th, this was the only store open on this block."

Added Willa Zakin Hallowell, a partner in a consulting firm, "People think this is a bookstore, but it's really a magic place."

Bohne said the disaster-relief experience lifted her spirits in the sense that everyday citizens realized "they could really do something" and were not rendered powerless by events.

Now that the need for immediate relief is subsiding, Bohne said, the Community Bookstore's emphasis is on providing information. "People need to stop hating each other and start paying attention," she said. "If they need help, they can call here."

As part of her continuing neighborhood outreach effort, Bohne recently persuaded author Sebastian Junger *(The Perfect Storm),* who has reported from Afghanistan, to address a neighborhood meeting. Although she had just two days notice to publicize Junger's reading from his new book, *Fire,* he drew a standing room-only crowd of 500 to the event.

Junger called Bohne again this week. The translator he employed while covering the conflict in Kosovo arrived in the United States and is looking for work, he said, and asked whether Bohne could help.

She's calling around.

> There's been an outbreak of kindness to strangers since September 11. So reports the *San Francisco Chronicle.* Three weeks after the attacks, yelling at the San Francisco towing company responsible for towing illegally parked cars is down from 80 percent to 30, and the California Highway Patrol reports road rage is off 15 percent.

CHAPTER 36

AP/Wide World Photos

PROTECT OUR NATION; PROTECT EACH OTHER

Dr. Fred H. Turpin

*I*t's been one week since I witnessed the attack on the World Trade Center in New York City. This Tuesday I went back into the city to work with people from a company that had lost more than 300 people in the attack. I went as a psychotherapist, as part of a volunteer effort to counsel these bereaved and devastated families. But there wasn't much counseling that could be done. Perhaps we were able to offer some words of comfort, to share their grief, to let them know the nation stood with them, to hear their stories, hold their hands.

One of the things that is difficult to imagine about this tragedy is that most of the victims were vaporized. Their offices had been on the floors of the North Tower where the impact occurred. The heat from the fireball was in excess of 2,000 degrees. There's not even any concrete from the collapse of the buildings—it was all pulverized. There's nothing but dust left.

I worked with teens today who had lost mothers, fathers, brothers, sisters, or other close family members. Most of the people who were killed were in their twenties and thirties. There were lots of babies in the room. And older people, too—there were many parents who had lost their children, often their only child. Some cried openly, but many just stared into open space or read the posters that were on the walls—hundreds of photographs of their loved ones, seeking information, seeking hope.

They had a meeting in a large conference room, and people were just weeping. One man wanted to know whether remains might be found and identified, because his kids insisted that he keep looking until they at least found something. Another wanted to know if they could be assured that their daughter died quickly, without much suffering. I just wanted to go around hugging people.

I volunteered, in part, because I couldn't stand the helplessness that seems to pervade almost every home. When the volunteer efforts are over, then I will walk downtown and witness for myself the gaping hole that is echoed in a thousand thousand hearts.

More people were killed in one hour than the United States lost in the entire Revolutionary War. Or at Pearl Harbor. Or on D-Day. I seem to need to hear those statistics. It helps me to measure the loss of human lives. But of course, those other losses were from military efforts. This was directed at people who were traveling or working in their offices. I cannot begin to fathom the minds of those who perpetrated this heinous act. But this is not a time to analyze their minds or motivations. Our first duty is to protect our nation and each other, our bridges and tunnels and harbors, our very way of life.

We sense that this will be a sea change for American society. Perhaps we will look back years from now and see this as the end of a Golden Age. On the other hand, some are saying that people just can't be so selfish anymore. That character is forged in adversity. That sacrifices will have to be made. Everyone is inspired by the heroic efforts of the fire and police departments. I think America will be stronger because of all of this.

David Letterman, on his first night back, spoke of the courage of the firefighters, the police, and Mayor Giuliani. He said that while few of us are capable of such courage, we can all pretend to be courageous. He was right. The line between courage and pretending to be courageous is very thin.

I encourage everyone to go into the city and be witness to this tragedy. Go see the wound and touch the city's pain. Before long, recovery efforts will be finished, but the excavation of the rubble will take almost a year before rebuilding efforts begin. While the wound is still open, it should become a shrine that every American should see.

The shock to the economy of the city will be severe. So see a show on Broadway. Have dinner at one of the fine restaurants. Encourage your friends not to cancel their trips or vacations to the city. Let us refuse to allow these acts of inhumanity to fill our lives with fear.

In a posting on AOL entitled "How Have You Changed?" as a consequence of the attacks, there was this entry:

Tonight, we invited all of our neighbors on our cul-de-sac to come out for an after dinner get-together on our driveway. We sat out until 11:00 just talking about everything that has happened and how it has affected us. In the end we all realized . . . that we need to be and do as we were and did before the events of September 11. We are Americans. . . . Don't let this affect the way we are; if we do, the terrorists have won a far greater victory. Talk to your neighbors, go to church, do not change your daily routine, and above all else, VALUE WHAT IT IS AND MEANS TO BE AN AMERICAN.

CHAPTER 37

AP/Wide World Photos

DOING GOOD FOR EACH OTHER

Cheryl Truman, *Lexington Herald-Leader*

*F*lags, flags everywhere, but what are we doing for each other? Yes, you've got an American flag flying somewhere: in front of your house, pasted to a window, waving from the antenna of your car. You're saddened. You're proud. You're angry. And you're showing it.

But what are you going to do about it?

First, stop pulling the car into the garage and disappearing into a cable TV cocoon of outrage and fear. Most of us aren't going to war. In fact, most of us won't come any closer to danger than a few minutes' more check-in time at the airport.

So let's think about what patriots do at times of national crisis. They do well by their patriotism by doing good for each other.

Consider this: Each individual who has a flag displayed on his or her home or car is challenged to perform one act of civic activism this week. For those of you who are unsure how to go about this, a few suggestions:

- Volunteer to build or clean up a neighborhood playground. One is being built at Dixie Elementary, another at Northern Elementary/Constitution Park [in Lexington, Kentucky]. And those are just the ones I know about because they're less than a mile from home. You've got a neighborhood park that likely could use a cleanup/spruce-up.

- Read to children at an elementary school or day care center. Offer to tutor slower readers. Donate money, time, or goods to your neighborhood school's Family Resource Center, which helps impoverished families remove barriers to learning. Offer to mow the grass for an elderly neighbor. Take a home-baked item to a neighbor who has done you a favor. Take a walk and learn the names of people you've seen around but have never met.

- Donate time and money to organizations such as the Humane Society; a Moveable Feast, which provides meals for AIDS patients; or the Hope Center, Lexington's hub for many of its homeless. Or volunteer for your church's outreach organization: Catholic Social Services and the United Methodist Church's Nathaniel Mission on DeRoode Street are two examples.
- Businesses flying the American flag are challenged to quietly donate goods to their area's impoverished or to the volunteer projects serving them.
- At the very least, don't throw cigarette butts out of your car while you're flying the flag. And don't affix an American flag sticker to your cell phone. That is *tacky* defined.
- Start a Neighborhood Watch. Some neighborhoods are blessed by having a cadre of senior citizen walkers on the streets from sunup to sundown; others are more yuppie-oriented, and need more organized protection.

CNN blares the theme: "America United." If we are united, shouldn't it be for more than fear? The old-fashioned American values include more than patriotic decor. They include building neighborhoods, looking out for your neighbor, and donating your time.

It's not just about the flag, after all.

> The Red Cross Club at Wilson High School in Long Beach, California, collected a series of poems, artwork, stories, and letters, put them together into a binder, and sent it to the victims of the World Trade Center attack.

TO DONATE MONEY

All proceeds from this book will be contributed to the American Red Cross and the NY Firefighters 9-11 Disaster Relief Fund. See page 201-202 for details on these organizations.

The September 11th Fund
United Way of New York City
2 Park Avenue
New York, NY 10016
Donate online: http://www.helping.org/wtc/11th.adp

> United Way and the New York Community Trust have created the September 11th Fund. Your contribution will be used to help with the immediate and longer-term needs of the victims, their families, and communities affected by the events of September 11. Launched with a $1 million donation from Williams Gas Pipeline, the Fund has received support from dozens of Fortune 500 companies and thousands of individuals.

The New York State World Trade Center Relief Fund
P.O. Box 5028
Albany, New York 12205
(800) 801-8092
International donors: 518-408-4992
Donate online: http://www.helping.org/wtc/ny/nystate.htm

If you would like to make a donation in person, please visit one of the following banks. Individuals with accounts at any of these banks can go to any of their branches within New York State, New Jersey, or Connecticut and make a donation to the Fund directly from their checking or savings account, credit card, or with cash.

JPMorganChase

Citibank

HSBC Bank USA

North Fork Bank

M&T Bank

Dime Savings Bank

GreenPoint Bank

Fleet Bank

The New York State World Trade Center Relief Fund was created when Governor George E. Pataki urged all New Yorkers and concerned Americans wishing to support the World Trade Center emergency response and victim support effort to contribute to the newly established fund.

The fund will be coordinated with the September 11th Fund, established by the United Way of New York City and the New York Community Trust, as well as the Twin Towers Fund established by the City of New York.

Twin Towers Fund
General Post Office
P.O. Box 26999
New York, NY 10087-6999
Donate online: http://www.helping.org/wtc/twin_towers.adp

Mayor Rudolph W. Giuliani has established the Twin Towers Fund to ensure that the generous outpouring of support for the families of our

uniformed service heroes affected by the disaster is coordinated, respon-
sive, responsible, and accountable. The purpose of the Twin Towers Fund is
to assist the families of the members of the uniformed services of the New
York City Fire Department and its Emergency Medical Services Command, the New York City Police Department, the Port Authority of New
York and New Jersey, the New York State Office of Court Administra-
tion, and other government offices who lost their lives or were injured
because of the tragedies of September 11, 2001, at the World Trade Center
in New York City.

If resources permit, the families of other persons who lost their lives or
were injured during the tragedies may also be included as beneficiaries.
The Twin Towers Fund will be administered by the New York City Public
Private Initiatives, Inc.

WTC Police Disaster Relief Fund

NYSFOP-Foundation 911 Police Plaza
Hicksville, NY 11801
Donate online: http://www.helping.org/wtc/wtcpdrf.adp
Please use tax ID Number 11-3207296

In response to the many inquiries offering assistance following the morning of September 11, 2001, the New York State Fraternal Order of Police
Foundation created the WTC Police Disaster Fund.

WTC School Relief Fund

"The Fund for Public Schools-WTC School Relief Fund"
110 Livingston Street, Room 826
Brooklyn, NY 11201
Donate online: http://www.helping.org/wtc/schoolrelief.adp

Many generous citizens of this great nation want to help the schoolchildren in New York City's Public School System in this time of crisis. In
response to this outpouring of concern, financial contributions are now

being accepted to help address the needs of the schoolchildren and schools affected by the World Trade Center tragedy.

AmeriCares

161 Cherry Street
New Canaan, CT 06840
Donate online: http://www.helping.org/wtc/americares.adp

AmeriCares, the national and international disaster relief organization, has established a fund for the spouses and children of those New York City uniformed firefighters, police officers, and Port Authority employees who have perished in the attacks. One hundred percent of all the donations to AmeriCares' "Heroes' Fund" will be distributed to the immediate families of the New York City firefighters, police officers, and Port Authority employees who have perished in this terrible tragedy.

Salvation Army National Corp

P.O. Box 269
615 Slaters Lane
Alexandria, VA 22313
Donate online: http://www.helping.org/wtc/sa.adp

The Salvation Army has been overwhelmed by offerings of supplies and materials for the relief efforts in New York and Washington, DC. Now monetary donations are needed to help pay for the 100,000 meals the Salvation Army is serving emergency personnel.

The American Society for the Prevention of Cruelty to Animals

424 East 92nd Street, 4th Floor
New York, NY 10128
Donate online: http://www.helping.org/wtc/aspca.adp

The American Society for the Prevention of Cruelty to Animals (ASPCA) is doing its best to help pet owners and animals during this time of need.

The ASPCA is the oldest humane organization in America, and was founded by Henry Bergh, a philanthropist and diplomat who recognized the inhumane treatment suffered by many animals in our society.

Engine Co. 22, Ladder Co. 13, 10th Battalion

Eng 22/Lad 13 Family Fund
Engine Co. 22/Ladder Co. 13
159 East 85th Street
New York, NY 10028

The Survivors' Fund—Washington DC Area

1112 16th Street, NW Suite 340
Washington, DC 20036
Donate online: http://www.helping.org/wtc/survivorsfund.adp

The Survivors' Fund focuses on the long-term educational, health, income maintenance, and other needs of individual victims and their families in the metropolitan Washington, DC, region, including the District of Columbia, Montgomery and Prince George's counties in Maryland, and communities in nearby Northern Virginia.

Robin Hood Foundation

111 Broadway, 19th Floor
New York, NY 10006
Donate online: http://www.helping.org/wtc/robinhood.adp

The Robin Hood Foundation fights poverty in New York City by applying investment principles to charitable giving. They fund the strongest, most effective poverty fighting organizations and leverage cash grants with in-depth management assistance. Every penny donated goes directly to the people who need it most, as Robin Hood's Board of Directors underwrites all administrative costs.

In response to the recent attack at the World Trade Center, Robin Hood has established the Robin Hood Relief Fund to aid in disaster relief in New York City. The Robin Hood Relief Fund will do what Robin Hood has always done—effectively help people in need. In particular, Robin Hood will work to ensure that the needs of lower income victims of the tragedy are met in both the immediate and long term.

The American Liberty Partnership

Some of the online crisis relief sites where Americans have donated directly to the charity of their choice, with no fees or costs, include:

Helping.org: An American Tragedy

Yahoo!: http://www.yahoo.com/

eBay: http://www.ebay.com

MSN: http://www.msn.com

AOL Keyword: How to Help

Amazon: http://www.amazon.com

On these Web sites, you will find opportunities to support organizations, as well as general information about how the relief effort is progressing and what needs are next on the horizon.

The Internet has played a strong role already in supporting the relief effort. In the first week alone, estimates are that more than $57 million was raised through online contributions at these Web sites to support charities involved in the relief efforts, much of it in donations of $30–$50 each.

The online medium has played an important role in other ways as well—connecting by e-mail and instant message friends and family members who couldn't reach one another by phone, providing real-time information about the disaster and its aftermath, and bringing a global community together to talk, share, and grieve.

The partners in the American Liberty Partnership believe that the online medium can continue to be a powerful tool to help rebuild our shattered communities and our shaken confidence. Working together, their goal is to provide convenient access to the best information and resources and to connect people with the philanthropic organizations most in need of our help.

Employee Funds of Affected Businesses

Following is a list of the most updated information on the employees of many of the companies in the World Trade Center towers, and the respective relief funds that have been established in their honor:

Aon Assistance Fund

c/o Harris Bank
36133 Treasury Center
Chicago, IL 60694-6100

Aon is a world leader in risk management, insurance brokerage, reinsurance, and human capital consulting services. As of September 21, Aon was still missing approximately 200 out of a total 1,100 employees. The Aon Assistance Fund has been established to aid the families of Aon employees who were injured or lost.

Cantor Fitzgerald Relief Fund

101 Park Avenue, 45th Floor
New York NY 10178-0060
Att: Dr. Phillip Ginsberg
Ms. Edie Lutnick
Donate online: http://www.helping.org/wtc/corporate_funds.adp#cantor

Cantor Fitzgerald is a leading treasury bond brokerage firm. As of September 21, they were missing more than 600 out of a total 1,000 employees. In response to this tragedy, Cantor Fitzgerald has set up this fund to provide emergency short-term financial assistance for the families of the victims, as well as ongoing assistance for childcare, college tuition, and long-term health care in the months and years ahead.

Carr Futures World Trade Center Memorial Fund

c/o The Northern Trust Company
50 South LaSalle Street
Chicago, IL 60675
Attn: Robin D. Levin, B-2
ABA # 071000152
Account number: 1893629
Swift code: CNORUS44
Wiring Instructions: Donations can be made in U.S. dollars or in any major currency. The Northern Trust Company will manage all currency conversions.

An international institutional brokerage firm, Carr Futures has confirmed the loss of one employee; with 69 still missing, and 71 accounted for as of September 21. This fund assists the families of its New York colleagues.

Euro Brokers/Maxcor Financial Group

The Euro Brokers Relief Fund
One New York Plaza, 16th Floor
New York, NY 10292-2011
Attn: Ruth Scharf

Maxcor Financial Group, Inc., and its Euro Brokers group company subsidiaries are leading domestic and international inter-dealer brokerage firms. As of September 21, one employee has been confirmed dead, with 59 still missing, out of a total of 285 employees.

Fiduciary Trust Company International

c/o Franklin Templeton Bank & Trust, FSB
One Franklin Parkway
San Mateo, CA 94403

Franklin Templeton Investments has established the FT Fiduciary Trust Memorial Fund to assist families affected by the tragedy. The company is issuing a $2 million challenge grant to its employees, and will be matching those contributions on a two-for-one basis. As of September 20, the firm has reported 90 of a total of 645 employees as missing.

Keefe, Bruyette & Woods

KBW Family Fund
North Fork Bank
275 Broad Hollow Road
Melville, NY 11747

Keefe, Bruyette, & Woods, a securities broker/dealer and investment bank, was missing 67 of their 171 employees as of September 21. The KBW Family Fund has been established for donations to assist the families of those KBW colleagues that are still missing or confirmed deceased as a result of the World Trade Center tragedy.

Marsh & McLennan Companies, Inc.

MMC Victims' Relief Fund
c/o MMC Public Affairs
1166 Avenue of the Americas, 4th Floor
New York, NY 10036

Leading global professional services firm, Marsh & McLennan Companies, Inc., was missing approximately 300 employees out of a total 1,700 as of September 21. MMC has established the MMC Victims' Relief Fund a charitable foundation to honor employees lost in these tragic events, and to contribute to the well-being of children and dependents who suffered loss. MMC will contribute $10 million to the fund and to other relief and recovery efforts.

Morgan Stanley

Morgan Stanley Victims Relief Fund
Morgan Stanley Community Affairs
1221 Avenue of the Americas, 27th Floor
New York, NY 10020

Preeminent global financial services firm, Morgan Stanley was missing 40 employees out of almost 3,500, according to reports on September 21.

Raytheon

Raytheon Employee Disaster Relief Fund/CCF
1445 South Figueroa Street, Suite 3400
Los Angeles, CA 90071-1638

Raytheon has established the Raytheon Employee Disaster Relief Fund to provide gifts from Raytheon and its employees to disaster relief for all victims. Raytheon is also providing disaster relief services through a grant the company made to the American Red Cross earlier this year.

As of September 24, Raytheon, a leading business and special mission aircraft manufacturer, has confirmed the loss of several employees on flights that crashed on September 11. A scholarship fund has been established for the children of Raytheon employees who were lost.

Sandler O'Neill & Partners

The Sandler O'Neill Assistance Foundation
P.O. Box 886
Chatham, NJ 07928

Friends of Sandler O'Neill & Partners, L.P., have established the Sandler O'Neill Assistance Foundation for the benefit of the victims of the World Trade Center tragedy and their families. In addition to Sandler O'Neill employees, this includes firefighters, police, and others who have worked so tirelessly and unselfishly on their behalf.

Sandler O'Neill & Partners, a full-service investment banking firm, has confirmed the loss of two employees as of September 23. Sixty-four employees are still listed as missing, while 111 of their total 177 employees have been accounted for. In addition, two of three company consultants are also listed as missing.

Windows of Hope Family Relief Fund
c/o David Berdon & Co., LLP
415 Madison Avenue
New York, NY 10017
http://www.windowsofhope.org

Windows of Hope Family Relief Fund has been established specifically for surviving family members and countless numbers of food industry personnel who worked throughout the huge complex in numerous corporate dining rooms and other small food service establishments. David Emil, owner of Windows on the World; the restaurant's executive chef, Michael Lomonaco; Tom Valenti, chef/owner Ouest Restaurant; and Waldy Malouf, chef/owner, Beacon Restaurant established the fund to be administered by J.P. Morgan Chase & Co. and David Berdon & Co., LLP. Checks should be made payable to Windows of Hope Family Relief Fund.

Family of Freedom Scholarship Fund
c/o CSFA
1505 Riverview Road
P.O. Box 297
St. Peter, MN 56082
Donate online: http://www.familiesoffreedom.org/

Families of Freedom Scholarship Fund has been established to help the children and spouses of the victims of the September 11, 2001 "Attack on America" realize their educational dreams. Former President Bill Clinton and Former Senate Majority Leader Bob Dole are backing the scholarship fund. Checks should be made payable to Citizens' Scholarship Fund of America (CSFA) designating "Families of Freedom Scholarship Fund" in the memo section.

Red Cross Planned Giving

Planned gifts include gifts through your will, charitable gift annuities, gifts of life insurance, pooled income funds, and charitable trusts.

Bequest

Many Red Cross supporters make charitable gifts by naming the Red Cross as a beneficiary in their wills.

Life Income Gift

You irrevocably transfer some assets to the Red Cross now, and in return, you (and a survivor, if you wish) receive income for life.

Gift of Life Insurance

If you no longer need your life insurance policy, you can donate it to the American Red Cross.

Pooled Income Fund

Your gift of money, marketable securities, or both is invested together with similar gifts from other supporters.

Charitable Lead Trust

Individuals with very large estates can use a charitable lead trust to benefit the American Red Cross and pass principal to family members with little or no tax penalty.

Gifts of Retirement Plans

Your IRA assets will be transferred to a charitable remainder trust, the trust will provide life income to the beneficiary, and then an eventual gift to the Red Cross.

To Give Blood

To find out where you can donate, visit *www.givelife.org* or call 1-800-GIVE-LIFE (1-800-448-3543).

Many generous Americans nationwide have been donating blood since the terrorist attacks September 11 to ensure a sustained and secure blood supply for all Americans. Together with the Red Cross, these blood heroes are ensuring that the safest possible blood is readily available whenever and wherever needed—for the military, for other blood centers in America and for all 5,000 of America's hospitals.

To Be a Tissue Donor

Call 1-888-4-TISSUE for more information.

Did you know that just one tissue donor can potentially benefit as many as fifty people? It's true. When you sign on to become a donor, your generous gift could bring many people new life.

Thanks to people like you, 600,000 lives have been enhanced since the establishment of American Red Cross Tissue services in 1982. However, the need for tissue continues to grow, and tissue such as skin for burn patients and certain sizes of heart valves for cardiac patients is in high demand.

Becoming a tissue donor is a simple, two-step process: first, sign a donor card or driver's license, and second, share your decision with your family, because next of kin is always asked for consent. There is no cost to you or your family. All costs related to tissue donation are paid for by the agency recovering the tissue.

(All major religions support tissue donation.) Recipients will not know who donated the tissue they receive. Selection is not based on race, sex, or ethnic origin, but rather on the medical need of the recipient. The identity of the donor is kept confidential.

Tissue donation will not interfere with a traditional funeral. Tissues are removed by people specifically trained for tissue recovery. The donor's body is handled with respect and dignity by the Red Cross. Tissue donation does not prohibit an open-casket funeral.

TO VOLUNTEER YOUR TIME

Red Cross
Yvonne Bell White
Volunteers, Youth, & Nursing
American Red Cross
431 18th Street, NW
Washington, DC 20006
Fax: (202) 639-3130
WhiteY@usa.redcross.org.

To Volunteer in Your Community
1-800-VOLUNTEER

To offer physical assistance, including fire, rescue and emergency medical services, please contact the NY State Volunteer Hotline for Fire and Medical Response at 1-800-801-8092

Online Resources

http://www.redcross.org/services/volunteer/opportunities/vol.html

http://www.firehouse.com/terrorist/fund.html

http://www.helping.org

http://www.libertyunites.org

http://www.citycares.org/national/

http://www.servenet.org

http://www.pointsoflight.org

http://www.unitedway.org

http://www.volunteermatch.org

To search on the Internet for your local volunteer center, type the name of your city.

FOR HELP COPING

The following is a list of valuable resources to help persons cope with the impact of disasters.

American Psychological Association
http://www.apa.org

National Institute of Mental Health
http://www.nimh.nih.gov

GriefNet
www.griefnet.org

Beliefnet
www.beliefnet.com

For Parents and Teachers

Online Resources

http://www.teacher.scholastic.com

http://www.parenting.com

http://www.education-world.com/a_curr/curr369.shtml

http://www.thirteen.org/teach/tips.html

http://www.extension.umn.edu/administrative/disasterresponse/terrorism.html

http://www.pta.org/parentinvolvement/tragedy/index.asp

http://www.nick.com/all_nick/specials/bighelp/helpamerica.jhtml

http://jfg.girlscouts.org/Talk/whoami/Issues/Action.htm#Top

http://www.nasponline.org/NEAT/crisis_0911.html

http://www.pbs.org/wnet/onourownterms/articles/children.html

http://www.nimh.nih.gov/publicat/violence.cfm

Just for Youth

It's easy to feel scared and helpless after a horrible event such as the September 11 terrorist attacks in America. The following tips may help you cope with the tragedy and help out others at the same time.

Speak out and be heard: Keep a journal of your thoughts and emotions. Write messages to the family and friends of the victims.

Hold a fundraiser: Raise money from your family, friends, and neighbors for rescue and relief organizations.

Send written expressions of sympathy and condolences: Not everyone can afford to send money or donate supplies, so some young people have been sending moral support instead. Show America's heroes you care by sending your thank-you notes, poems, and drawings for rescue workers. Mail your messages to the addresses following.

For New York City, mail to:

Kids Care Clubs Helping Hands Kids Care Clubs
Points of Light Foundation
382 Smith Ridge Road
South Salem, NY 10590

For Washington, D.C., mail to:

Kids Care Clubs Helping Hands Kids Care Clubs
Points of Light Foundation
1400 Eye Street NW, Suite 800
Washington, D.C. 20005

U.S. Fund for UNICEF
Attn: "Kids Helping Kids"
333 East 38th Street, 6th Floor
New York, NY 10016

Workers from UNICEF will personally deliver your messages to the children.

TIME For Kids
Kids' Collages for Heroes
P.O. Box 5175
Rockefeller Center
New York, NY 10185-5175
Express Yourself Online: New York Firefighters
http://www.iaff.org/across/911/form/default.asp

Online Resources

http://www.theangelproject.com/

http://www.youthnoise.com

http://www.servenet.org

http://www.volunteermatch.org

http://www.helping.org

http://www.nik.com

http://www.pbs.org/wgbh/zoom/

THANK YOU FOR YOUR COURAGE TO GIVE

*C*ompiling this book in such a short period of time with such deeply felt emotion has been an amazing experience, one I'll forever cherish. The old African proverb "It takes a village to raise a child" is the only reasonable explanation for this book. The support, energy, and hours of hundreds of people—all donating their services—gave this book its wings.

America, September 11 would not be possible without my collaborators, Brenda Welchlin and Karen Frost. Their talents, expertise, and tireless efforts made a vision a reality. Thanks to Brenda, journalist extraordinaire, for giving her superb writing talents and heart to this book. And thanks to Mark, Keeton, Haven, and Zach for supporting her absence from their lives for two weeks. Thanks to Karen, my longtime publicist and very dear friend, for her help. Every media outlet in the country responded to her requests for reprints, waiving fees and expediting the process due to her compassionate beliefs and her bulldog persistence. And special thanks to Hogan, the long red dog, for providing Karen much needed comic relief during this process.

I'm deeply grateful to my editor and friend, Mary Jane Ryan, whose brilliant editing and loving support blessed this project.

My gratitude extends to my agent, Jim Levine, for seeing my vision, understanding the healing power of giving, and immediately taking action to make this happen. Special thanks to my family at Conari Press—Suzanne Albertson, Leslie Berriman, Jenny Collins, Will Glennon, Julie Kessler, Brenda Knight, Rosie Levy, Everton Lopez, Heather McArthur, Don McIlraith, Brian Reed, Leah Russell, Mignon Freeman, Claudia Smelser, Pam Suwinsky—for committing to publish yet another book that helps build a better world. Thanks, also, to Michael Fine, Kaethe Fine, and Stanley Last at MJF Books, Fine Communications, for their support and story leads. I would also like to extend my heartfelt thanks and gratitude to the following other organizations who were pleased and proud to have participated in this project: Domtar in Nekoosa, Wisconsin, for the donation of the 55# Westminster Tradebook paper; Embassy Graphics in Winnipeg, Manitoba, Canada, for the cover preparation and film; and Jaguar Advanced Graphics in Bethpage, New York for the cover printing.

Thanks to the media outlets in our country who so graciously gave permission to reprint their stories of courage and hope. A special thank you to all of the volunteer Web sites for information needed for the resource guide.

Many thanks to my friend, Saunders, the computer wizard, for her patience in teaching me how to use Microsoft Word and how to initiate successful searches on the Internet, and to Mitch Nielson at Binion.com for adding information on this book to my Website. Thanks to Dee, Dana, and Mary Ellen "Angelscribe" for lending their wisdom, talent, and experience.

I am forever grateful for my family—my precious husband of twenty-nine years, Steve; our children Melissa, Todd, and Michael; and our dachshund, Johnnie—for always giving me perspective with their love, light, and laughter.

A thank you to friends and family who understand my mission and take up the slack for me all too often—Sarah, Jack, Maxine, Ellen, Tommy, Holly, Mike, Carol, Howard, Cherie, Neal, Cindy, Alan, Judy, Barry, Marcy, Lew,

Bart, Stacey, Lexie, Irma, and Juanita. And a special thanks to Marvin and Erwin.

Thank you to my doctor, Dr. Jonathan Walker, for helping to keep me healthy in body, mind, and spirit.

To the contributors of this book—those who graciously contributed original stories: Thank you. Because of your willingness to contribute to this book, we all will experience the miracles that occur when we have the courage to give.

To all of those around the world who have given your time, expertise, funds, prayers, tears, and thoughts to the rescue efforts—your courage to give—our country thanks you.

To those of you who have lost dear ones, our heartfelt thoughts and prayers extend to you. And finally, to the victims of this tragedy, we acknowledge you. We pledge to honor you by finding our courage to give now and always.

—Jackie Waldman

Thanks to the following people for their original contributions to *America, September 11:*

Kathleen Avino

Cindy Bahnij

Susan C. DeMerit

Helen Engelhardt

William Harvey

Larry Hawk

Kaitlin Kisela

Jason Kordelos

Ms. Mac

Linda Mason

Caren Messing

Omar Tesdell

Dr. Fred H. Turpin

Annie Wignell

Thanks for permission to excerpt from the previously published works: Chapter 1: Copyright ©2001, *Milwaukee Journal Sentinel.* Reprinted by permission; Chapter 4: Reprinted with permission of the *Dallas Morning News;*

Who This Book Will Benefit

With deeply felt gratitude for the many heroic efforts, lifesaving services rendered, and relief provided to victims of the disaster, we donate all proceeds of *America, September 11: The Courage to Give* to the American Red Cross and the New York Firefighters 9-11 Disaster Relief Fund.

THE AMERICAN RED CROSS

Send checks payable to "The American Red Cross" to:

American Red Cross
P.O. Box 37243
Washington, DC 20013
800-HELP NOW or 800-257-7575 (Spanish)
Donate online: http://www.redcross.org

$600 buys food for a week and clothing for a family of four.

$300 buys five days of meals and motel stays for one displaced disaster victim.

$250 provides emergency shelter and food for fifty disaster victims for one day.

$100 buys replacement prescription medication, like insulin, blood pressure, or seizure medication for three disaster victims who have lost everything.

$50 buys ten new blankets in an emergency.

NEW YORK FIREFIGHTERS 9-11 DISASTER RELIEF FUND

Send checks payable to "The New York Firefighters 9-11 Disaster Relief Fund" to:

New York Firefighters 9-11 Disaster Relief Fund
P.O. Box 65858
Washington DC 20035-5858 or
Donate online: http://www.helping.org/wtc/iaff.adp
Wire the money at ABA # 026 003 379 and bank account # 846 011 67.

In the wake of the September 11 tragedy, the International Association of Fire Fighters (IAFF) is preparing to send financial assistance to the families of all fallen firefighters and to coordinate efforts to assist fire and EMS personnel on the scene in New York City. This assistance is in the form of the New York Firefighters 9-11 Disaster Relief Fund.

"The International and its members are mourning the loss of our brothers and sisters," said General President Schaitberger. "There will be many funds established to help the victims. We are encouraging our members to ask other friends of the fire service to donate to the New York Firefighters 9-11 Disaster Relief Fund. This money will go directly to the families of the fallen fire fighters and EMS personnel in New York City."

"This fund is the only one directly affiliated with the IAFF, the Uniformed Firefighters Association of New York, Local 94 and the New York Uniformed Fire Officer Association, Local 854," Schaitberger continued. "Our brothers and sisters appreciate this generosity."

"In the aftermath of this tragedy, the families of our fallen brothers and sisters shouldn't have to worry about money," said Vinnie Bollon, General Secretary-Treasurer of the IAFF. "The New York Firefighters 9-11 Disaster Relief Fund will make sure they get the assistance they need."

*J*ackie Waldman was living the "perfect life" with three healthy children, a loving husband, and a thriving business when she discovered she had multiple sclerosis. Instead of dwelling on her physical pain, she used that energy to begin a new career in volunteerism. Jackie co-founded Dallas' Random Acts of Kindness™ Week. She has appeared twice on *Oprah!*, and was chosen by CNN as one of their Millennium Heroes. She is a recipient of the 1999 Girls, Inc., "She Knows Where She's Going" Award.

The author of three books, *The Courage to Give, Teens with the Courage to Give,* and the upcoming *Teachers with the Courage to Give,* Jackie inspires others to give through volunteering—no matter what—and to discover that they, too, can triumph over tragedy to make a difference in the world.

Jackie serves as a spokesperson for Biogen, Inc.—a global biopharmaceutical company principally engaged in discovering and developing drugs for human health care through genetic engineering and winner of the U.S. National Medal of Technology—and AVONEX® (Interferon beta-1a), a treatment of relapsing forms of multiple sclerosis.

She lives in Dallas, Texas, with Steve, her husband of twenty-nine years; three children, Melissa, Todd, and Michael; and miniature dachshund Johnnie.

For more information about Jackie Waldman, volunteer opportunities, and the subject of her books, visit her Web site at *http://www.couragetogive.com.*

*B*renda Welchlin has reported and edited for both small weekly newspapers and metropolitan dailies. After almost a decade of breathing newsroom air, most recently at the *Dallas Morning News* and the *Des Moines Register,* she traded in regular deadlines to write and edit projects from home and spend more time with her family. She worked out of the 93rd floor of the World Trade Center during election week in November 2000 as the Iowa state manager for Voter News Service. She holds degrees in journalism, math, and sociology from Texas Christian University in Fort Worth, Texas, and was a Fulbright Scholar at the University of Christchurch in New Zealand. Currently she lives in Ames, Iowa, with her family: Mark, Keeton, Haven, and Zach.

*K*aren Frost is principal and owner of Frost Media Relations, a public relations consulting firm, which she founded in 1998. She is a full-time media relations consultant, entrepreneur, and speaker/facilitator for Courage to Give(tm) Workshops to corporations, schools, and nonprofits around the country. Prior to launching her own agency, Karen was director of publicity for a national publishing company, worked on the political advertising team for Senator Ted Kennedy, Congressman Richard Gephardt, and former Speaker of the House Tom Foley, freelanced for CBS News and Fox News Service, and managed the pressroom for the Perot 1992 campaign in Dallas, Texas. Karen also worked in Uganda, East Africa, for Habitat for Humanity. Although a Texan at heart, she currently lives in Alexandria, Virginia, with her long red dog, Hogan.

Workshop Opportunities

Finding Your Courage to Give is a workshop program specially designed for corporations, schools, and nonprofit organizations. The process allows an individual to discover his or her "giving style" and provides the necessary tools, according to each individual's uniqueness, to create an action plan to volunteer. The skills developed in the workshop also enhance an organization's group dynamics as the individuals gain a deeper understanding of others and improve their communication skills. *Finding Your Courage to Give* workshops allow organizations to enrich participants' personal lives, strengthen their culture within, and give to the community around them. For more information, contact Karen Frost at (214) 373-6267 or *kfrost@couragetogive.com*.

Speaking

If you are interested in Jackie Waldman speaking to your organization, contact Karen Frost at (214) 373-6267 or *kfrost@couragetogive.com*.

To Our Readers

Conari Press publishes books on topics ranging from spirituality, personal growth, and relationships to women's issues, parenting, and social issues. Our mission is to publish quality books that will make a difference in people's lives—how we feel about ourselves and how we relate to one another. We value integrity, compassion, and receptivity, both in the books we publish and in the way we do business.

As a member of the community, we donate our damaged books to nonprofit organizations, dedicate a portion of our proceeds from certain books to charitable causes, and continually look for new ways to use natural resources as wisely as possible.

Our readers are our most important resource, and we value your input, suggestions, and ideas about what you would like to see published. Please feel free to contact us, to request our latest book catalog, or to be added to our mailing list.

2550 Ninth Street, Suite 101
Berkeley, California 94710-2551
800-685-9595 510-649-7175
fax: 510-649-7190
e-mail: conari@conari.com
www.conari.com